CATHE

MEDITATIONS

CATHEDRAL MEDITATIONS

Joan Bristow

TRIANGLE

*To all my relatives and friends
who have meditated with me
on this pilgrimage*

★

First published in Great Britain in 1998 by
SPCK
Holy Trinity Church
Marylebone Road
London NW1 4DU

The author and publisher acknowledge with thanks permission to
reproduce part of 'All Heaven Declares' by Noel Richards and
Tricia Roberts. Copyright © 1987 Kingsway's Thankyou Music,
PO Box 75, Eastbourne, East Sussex, BN23 6NW, UK.

Bible quotations are from the New International Version
© 1973, 1978 and 1984 by the International Bible Society.
Published by Hodder & Stoughton, unless
otherwise stated, when they are from the Authorized Version,
which is the property of the Crown in perpetuity.

British Library Cataloguing-in-Publication Data

A catalogue record for this book is available from
the British Library

ISBN 0-281-05095-3

Typeset by Pioneer Associates Ltd, Perthshire
Printed in Great Britain by
Caledonian International, Glasgow

CONTENTS

CONTENTS

PREFACE

Our English Anglican cathedrals have attracted many thousands of people over the centuries, originally as places of pilgrimage, nowadays for a variety of reasons. For students of architecture, they are invaluable. In terms of historical interest, there is a wealth of fascinating detail to discover.

I have always been drawn to them myself, although never fully understanding why. When visiting these magnificent buildings I have conscientiously studied the guidebooks, endeavouring not to miss any detail of architecture or history outlined in them. Or I have followed guides, trying to absorb every piece of information they have given as I walked with them through the nave, aisles, transepts, choir and chapels. However, inevitably when I have done this I have come away without much feeling of spiritual uplift. I have therefore decided, in visiting our cathedrals, to concentrate instead on seeking out something that speaks to me with some kind of spiritual significance, and I have not been disappointed. At times this has come through a particular experience whilst in the cathedral; at other times it has simply come in the thoughts I have had as I have studied some of its features.

Time is often limited when making these visits, particularly on coach tours. Rather than trying to take in every detail, therefore, I invite the reader to accompany me on my 'pilgrimage', to meditate with me on what a cathedral has to say that is of spiritual value, and to pray with me in a quiet place.

There are over 40 Anglican cathedrals in England, and this book covers just half of them. My prayer is that visitors may perhaps also find their own special place as they tour these great houses built for the glory of God, and maybe even feel prompted to make one or more return visits.

Joan Bristow

INTRODUCTION

1

CHICHESTER

To know, to love, to follow

Like many English cathedrals, the one in Chichester is situated right in the heart of the city, in the centre of business, shopping, education and all that makes up everyday living. It has stood on this site since Norman times, although each time-span, including the twentieth century, has added something to its structure. The 277-foot (84-metre) spire, clearly visible from miles away, and the detached fifteenth-century bell tower have therefore always been at the centre of life here.

Just inside the entrance, to our left and on the north side, is a small chapel known as the Sailors' Chapel, dedicated as a memorial to the men of Sussex who lost their lives at sea in World War II. One window here portrays the story of Jesus walking on the water. He is shown putting out his arms and taking hold of his disciple Simon Peter, who has tried to walk to Jesus but, having taken his eyes off his master, has begun to sink. The words of Jesus to his disciple in that story come to us: 'You of little faith, why did you doubt?'[1] How much faith do we have, if any? Perhaps we have looked away from Jesus, and may therefore be experiencing a sense of insecurity.

We wander along the north aisle, past the kinds of memorials and tombs that are usually associated with cathedrals, until we reach the Bell-Arundel screen that separates the choir from the nave. As we walk across to the south aisle, we glimpse, through this great screen, the modern John Piper tapestry behind the high altar, with its theme of the Holy Trinity.

We turn into the south transept where, even on a dull day, the glorious colours of the enormous window here are so brightened by the light from outside that we gasp at their beauty. The window shows, at the top, Christ seated in glory, a brilliant blue cloak over his white robe. Such a picture calls for our worship and, when we examine the rest of the window, we begin to understand why.

Here, in this window, we can trace the full gospel story. Down at the right-hand side we see Adam and Eve being expelled from the Garden of Eden, having disobeyed God, portraying our concept of original sin. Other scenes show various events in the Old Testament writings, such as the stories of Abraham, Moses and others. Then we move on to those of the New Testament, including the Annunciation scene, the infant Jesus being taken to the temple, his baptism in the River Jordan by John the Baptist, the Last Supper with his disciples, and his death on the cross.

The whole gospel is seen here in a way that illiterate people could readily understand in the past. Humanity sinned and, throughout the ages, that sin continued. So God, loving the world he had created, made a plan. He would send his Son, Jesus Christ, to die for the sins of the world. Jesus fulfilled that purpose in his earthly life; God raised him from death and received him back to his side where he now reigns in glory.

The window, however, does not show us all the details that emphasize why we should worship Christ for what he did, and we must move on towards the retrochoir for a more in-depth understanding.

On the way, in the south choir aisle, we pause in front of two twelfth-century stone panels, considered to be the two greatest artistic treasures of this cathedral. These Romanesque carvings show two scenes from a story in John's Gospel: Christ arriving at Bethany and being greeted by Mary and Martha, and the raising of Lazarus from death.[2] The sorrow expressed in the faces is very marked, particularly of Jesus, and we realize the depth of his grief.

From here it is just a few steps to the retrochoir, which is the crucial point of pilgrimage to Chichester. Here is the site of the shrine of St Richard, who was Bishop of Chichester during the thirteenth century and is probably the best known of all those associated with this cathedral. He was revered for his great love and concern for the poor, which won him the title of the 'model diocesan bishop'. His statue stands to one side of the platform, which is also the burial place of George Bell, a well-loved bishop of more recent times, known particularly for his work for German refugees during the last world war. It seems so appropriate then, that, because of Bishop Bell's links with the German churches, the gigantic tapestry at the back of the platform here is called the Anglo-German tapestry. It was designed by Ursula Benker-Schirmer and the weaving was done both in Sussex and Bavaria. It speaks of reconciliation between peoples, but, at a deeper level, of the reconciliation between God and individual men and women, made possible because of the death of Jesus.

At first sight, the tapestry startles us with the complexity of its shapes and colours, but a close scrutiny is well worth while. There are four main symbols: the candle, fig tree, fish and – St Richard's special symbol – the chalice. Right at the heart of the chalice is seen the cross. Other symbols in the design are the dove, representing the Holy Spirit; the triangle, a sign of the Trinity; the serpent, reminding us of evil and temptation; and the lotus supporting the chalice.

We may feel the overall picture is harsh, but surely there could be nothing more harsh than the situation that faced Jesus as he prayed in the Garden of Gethsemane for the 'cup' he realized the Father had given him to drink to be taken from him. If he followed where he knew God was leading him, ahead stood a cross, the Roman gallows of the day, where he would be nailed by his hands and feet and left to die. Little wonder he prayed that, if it were possible, the cup should be taken from him. But the climax of his prayer – 'My Father, if it is not possible for this cup to be taken away unless I drink it, may your will be done'[3] – has given Christians reason to rejoice ever since. He did indeed drink that cup to its bitter last drops, and triumphantly.

3

Because he did so, we can know complete forgiveness and reconciliation with God, when we repent and accept this in faith.

The message of the tapestry gives us the full reason for our worshipping Christ, who now reigns in glory. Although he was divine, he allowed himself to suffer torture, desolation and the most cruel death imaginable, as a man, in order that the world – and each individual in it – might find salvation. The tapestry conveys this message eloquently.

In front of the platform is a small stand containing copies of the prayer of St Richard, written so many years ago and yet still so well known and used, even to the point of being adapted in the modern musical *Godspell*. We can pick up a card freely to read and take away. St Richard prays:

> Thanks be to Thee, my Lord Jesus Christ,
> For all the benefits which Thou hast given me,
> For all the pains and insults which Thou hast borne for me.
> O most merciful Redeemer, Friend, and Brother,
> May I know Thee more clearly,
> Love Thee more dearly
> And follow Thee more nearly.

As we meditate on this well-loved prayer, we realize that in these words we have found a three-fold purpose for visiting this and other cathedrals.

By the time Jesus came to earth, the Israelites thought they knew God, although many felt him to be a vengeful God, a God of wrath and fierce anger, a God who punishes, a God who judges. Although we have to acknowledge that those are some aspects of God's nature, they are only part of the picture. Indeed, the Old Testament writers also wrote of a God of compassion, tenderness, deep understanding; a God who is merciful, who provides for and leads his people, but, above all, a God who is mighty, powerful and glorious. In Jesus we see all this to a magnificent degree.

- In Jesus we see light and truth.
- In Jesus we see the compassion that stooped at once to

minister to someone's need whenever he came across it.

- In Jesus we see a complete understanding of what goes on within the heart of a person and, because of that insight, he could go right to the root of the problem and help in a unique way.
- In Jesus we see anger at hypocrisy.
- In Jesus we see love that surpasses any love we can ever know, however intimate our human relationships may be. Above all, we see the ultimate love of God, who sent Jesus into the world in order to save it.

These are the kinds of attributes brought to mind here, and it is through these portrayals that we find in glass, stone, statue, painting, tapestry, carved wood and so on that we can know him 'more clearly'.

As people such as Simon Peter, Mary, Martha and Lazarus got to know Jesus more clearly, so their love for him grew. In the same way, many others have learned to love him 'more dearly'. With that love has come a great desire to follow him 'more nearly', which some have done at the cost of their lives; while many still follow and find true fulfilment and the purpose for living.

In most cathedrals there is a place set aside for private prayer, and here in Chichester that place is the lady chapel, which is behind us as we stand looking at the tapestry. If we really want to know God better, to love him more deeply and to follow him faithfully, prayer is where we begin. Whether our tradition is to kneel or simply to sit with bowed head, we can be free to adopt whatever attitude is right for us, as we pray from our hearts.

The prayer of St Richard can be our starting-point as we sit here quietly in Chichester's lady chapel. On the visits to other cathedrals described later, the meditations will follow different aspects of the last three lines of St Richard's prayer.

Lord God, as we admire the creative work of those who raised buildings to your glory, we praise you for your creation of our world. Most of all, we give you praise and thanks for sending your Son,

Jesus Christ, to die for our world and all who are in it. Help us to understand more of what this means and to accept this tremendous demonstration of your love. Then, as we understand more, may our love for you grow daily.

In response to your love, and as an expression of our love for you, may your Holy Spirit show us how we can follow you in our everyday living.

May the memory of our visit here remain strong in our minds, and our desire to serve you increase.

Amen

Before we leave the cathedral and return to the busyness of everyday living, we step out into the cloisters from the south aisle, turn to our left and look up at St Richard's porch. Above the double arch, we see another statue of him and remember how he learned to know, love and follow God supremely.

PART I

To know thee more clearly

2

DERBY

From everlasting to everlasting

As we approach Derby Cathedral, the great medieval 200-foot (61-metre) tower that dominates the city suggests we are about to enter a familiar style of building. So we are all the more startled when we walk inside to find one as unlike a traditional cathedral as we could imagine. An exclamation of 'It's so different' brings a smile to the face of the volunteer guide, who tells us that our reaction is the same as that of most visitors. In fact, it would be understandable if we thought we had made a mistake and come to the wrong place, for it is small, rectangular and plain inside, with mainly clear glass windows, light stone walls and plain pillars, giving a very light and airy appearance. Even the screen separating nave and choir is different, being made of wrought iron. The impression is of a modern building but, in fact, it is more than 200 years old, having replaced an earlier structure.

Our eyes are drawn to the two windows that are of stained glass, described in our guidebook as 'glimpses of a primordial struggle between darkness and light'. The modern, abstract designs in brilliant blues and golds represent the two traditional concepts of All Souls and All Saints, referring to the cathedral's dedication.

Passing along the north aisle and reaching the Consistory Court, we look up at the All Souls window, dark and sombre, a symbol of the struggle of the human soul to emerge from its physical limitations. And crossing in front of the screen, we come to that part of the cathedral now known as the Cavendish Area, where the All Saints window sheds light and clarity,

9

depicting the achievement of the soul's spiritual consummation. In this area also we admire a lovely little statue of the Madonna and child, as well as a traditional type of stone font.

Immediately outside this area we spot a steep and narrow stairway and descend to discover a place with a completely different atmosphere. This small crypt chapel was converted from part of a burial vault in 1978, and it has retained an earlier dedication to St Katharine, the fourth-century saint who is said to have been tortured on a wheel. In fact, the wheel is seen in the design of the kneelers here.

This peaceful little chapel, which can probably seat no more than a dozen worshippers, was initially provided as a quiet place for private prayer. It is also used for services during the week and there is an aumbry for the reserved sacrament. The consecration of this place meant that the cathedral had a second altar, something that had been missing for many years.

The chapel has an almost cave-like feel about it, a reminder of the Garden Tomb in Jerusalem where it is said the body of Jesus was laid after the crucifixion. That death on the cross is strikingly recalled here by a bronze crucifix, made in modern style by a local artist, and this is also used as a Lenten processional cross. It hangs above an altar made from Derbyshire marble, and it is what the marble contains that captures our attention. In it are plant-like fossils, probably sea-lilies, for the marble is crinoidal. They were really primitive animals living about 340 million years ago. The whole marble slab seems, in fact, to show a myriad of fossils of small sea creatures. Looking at those fossils of so long ago, and the modern representation of the crucifixion above that altar, a verse from Psalms comes to mind: 'From everlasting to everlasting you are God'.[1]

So much research is carried out to try to establish just how and when the universe evolved, and many different theories have been propounded. Some people completely dismiss the idea of God being the creator, while others cling tenaciously to the account in the first chapter of Genesis in the Bible, of him creating the heavens and the earth 'in the beginning'.[2]

In our quest to know God better, we have, of course, to acknowledge his existence. A verse in the New Testament has a very common-sense point of view. It says quite simply that anyone who wants to please God and who comes to him 'must believe that he exists and that he rewards those who earnestly seek him'.[3] It goes without saying that it is little use wanting to know God better if we do not believe in him. That belief is the beginning of our faith. It is a fundamental consciousness and certainty that there is an all-powerful being who created the universe. That faith accepts that he made the world, not by manufacturing it in any kind of way, but simply by calling it into being.

The great hymn of praise at the beginning of our Bibles was wrung from the heart of someone looking about at the world and seeing a mighty hand at work in it and behind it, an all-powerful being, an orderly pattern conceived by a unique mind, who continues his creative activity even today. And this writer simply attributed it all to God. He was not interested in any scientific explanations about the existence of matter and so on or how these things came into being. His faith began and ended with God, whom he believed had always existed as the great I Am. The psalm quoted earlier echoes this thought.

- The power behind the universe has always been God, throughout all generations.
- This power was God before any mountains were raised, before volcanic activity, earthquakes, tornadoes.
- This God was the power that brought order out of chaos, establishing earth and sea, giving light.
- This same God detailed the minute cell-like life as well as the gigantic creatures we think existed in prehistoric times.
- This same God added beauty and colour with plant life and great trees.
- It was this same God who created human beings in his own image, and set them to be stewards in the beautiful world he had made.

It calls for a tremendous act of faith to take all that on board, to listen to all that the scientists tell us, accepting perhaps much of what they say, finding interest in their theories, while at the same time seeing behind it all the mighty power of God working in his unique way with magnificent creativity. It is a mystery, however convincing are the explanations we are given, and are still being given, as new discoveries are constantly being brought to light. Of greater mystery, perhaps, is the spoiling of this wonderful creation, and for that we have to blame humanity.

The amazing thing about whoever wrote that first chapter of Genesis is that the author lived in the same world in which we live, yet was able to end the chapter with the all-inclusive words: 'God saw all that he had made, and it was very good.'[4] Here is a thought to cheer our hearts when, looking at the world of today, we see gloom and doom; our faith tells us that initially God made this world good. And it was because it was meant to be good that Jesus came. He is described as 'the same yesterday and today and for ever'.[5] It is this same Jesus who is also accredited with making and sustaining everything in the universe, for he is one with God.

Here in this tiny underground chapel we feel this great and unchanging truth of the God who has always been, and who always will be, from ancient times right through to our own day and age, and beyond. If anything can rid us of a feeling of insecurity, surely this thought can do so.

Everlasting God, before we leave the quietness of this small chapel, we bow before your awesomeness, praising you especially because the past, present and future all belong to you.

Our praise is also for Jesus, known in the New Testament as the Word, through whom all things were made and through whom they are still sustained.

Our praise continues for your Holy Spirit, who was there at the beginning of creation, and who is around us always, giving strength, teaching, convincing and comforting us, as well as making us aware of those things we do that are wrong.

We pray, Lord God, for your forgiveness when we doubt, and ask that you will show us the answer to our questions, that we may trust you more and more as our relationship with you grows through a deeper knowledge of yourself.
Help us to see your hand in nature and as we go about the world you have created, and help us to respect your great creation.
We acknowledge that you have been our help in ages past and that you are our hope for years to come, for a thousand years in your sight are like but a day. Help us to so number our days aright that 'we may gain a heart of wisdom'.[6]
Amen

We return to the main part of this unusual cathedral and cross back to the north side, pausing beside something even more modern. Standing just here, ready to be moved to a place where it can be seen by all the congregation, is a stainless steel portable font, dedicated and first used on Mothering Sunday in 1987. This was made by a group of Rolls-Royce undergraduate apprentices, as an addition to their training, to celebrate the cathedral's diamond jubilee. It stands here in sharp contrast to the more traditional font we saw earlier in the Cavendish Area.

The phrase 'ancient and modern' comes readily to mind in this cathedral and, however old-fashioned that phrase may seem, it is a cue that the God we seek to know more clearly is the God of both.

3

WINCHESTER

Order out of chaos

When visiting our cathedrals, it is often obvious that there are particular plans for the day. They are not kept locked, only to be used for special occasions. These great buildings are still in constant use and not only on Sundays or for other recognized services. When planning a visit we have, therefore, to be prepared to find crowds gathering, as well as various distractions. Parts of the nave may even be hung with modern and colourful banners, and there can be much activity.

Winchester Cathedral is no exception, as it is a magnificent setting for festivals and concerts, and well-known orchestras are welcomed here. During a rehearsal for an evening's concert, however, the tuning-up process of the instrumentalists does not really seem conducive to a quiet spiritual experience in a house of God. The truth is, of course, that God can speak to our hearts above the noise and clamour, as we shall discover.

The beautiful little Epiphany Chapel in the north transept, although set aside for private prayer, does not guarantee that the sound of orchestral tuning-up will not be heard. Despite this, we cannot fail to be impressed by the four colourful windows showing crucial episodes in the life of the Virgin Mary around the time of the birth of Jesus: the Annunciation, her visit to Elizabeth, the Nativity scene and, above the simple altar, the Adoration of the Magi.

To reach this chapel, we have passed, *en route*, the grave and memorial window of Jane Austen, the novelist, and glanced across the nave to other interesting windows and memorials, including that to the memory of Isaak Walton, the famous angler.

14

When scheduled events are taking up space in cathedrals, however, it is not always possible to examine the many interesting details around the ancient walls.

Though there may be some commotion and distractions, we can move away from the centre of the activity to the retrochoir to find the modern monument to St Swithun, the well-known ninth-century saint forever associated with rain and connected with this cathedral. His memorial is very impressive, although there is one in this area to look out for that is much more modest. It is to a man who, but for his efforts, there would be no cathedral standing here today. His name was William Walker, and the small modern statue that commemorates his work stands near the lady chapel. The inscription tells us he was a diver 'who saved this cathedral with his two hands'.

It was not until the beginning of the twentieth century that it was realized the east end of the cathedral was in danger of collapsing because the foundations were subsiding. The dean and chapter therefore decided that the walls must be underpinned, but as this was difficult because of the high level of the water table, a brilliant idea was hit on by a consultant engineer, Francis Fox. Why not use a deep-sea diver to do the work? Before that could happen, labourers were employed to dig deep trenches below the walls of the cathedral until the rising ground-waters made excavation impossible, and then the diver took over.

First, Walker dug out the raft of beech logs on which the retrochoir had been founded. Then he laid a firm foundation of sacks of cement concrete, working entirely by feel. He continued until nearly the whole cathedral was underpinned by this method. It took him at least five years, spending six hours a day working in up to 20 feet (6 metres) of muddy water. About 150 workmen were employed on the project, but William Walker is the one remembered for saving the whole cathedral from collapse. Unfortunately, though, because of a misunderstanding, the commemorative statuette was modelled on the consultant engineer, Francis Fox, but surely the two men can be honoured for their

15

particular work in saving the structure. Despite their efforts, in bad weather the crypt is still known to flood.

It is clearly vitally important to have a firm and solid foundation for such a magnificent edifice. Even more vital is it to have a firm and solid foundation for our faith, which will be as a rock when we pass through treacherous times and feel we may sink. This thought is still in our minds as we walk down the south choir aisle towards the presbytery, to stand in front of the high altar with the great screen behind it. Although this magnificent screen was built in the latter part of the fifteenth century, the original intricate carvings in fine-grained limestone were broken up at the time of the Reformation and so the present statues date from the late nineteenth century.

High up is a crucifix, as we would expect, with Mary and the apostle John on either side looking up at Christ as he hangs on the cross. This in itself is eye-catching. Standing as near to the altar as possible our gaze, too, is directed up at him, although it is the section immediately below the crucifix, showing the beginning of Jesus' earthly life, that gives us a spiritual uplift.

On a sunny day, a sudden shaft of clear sunlight from a high window lights up a clear representation of the manger scene. Among the sculpted figures are seen Mary and Joseph with the baby Jesus, simply that – no haloes or angels, no shepherds or wise men. The sunlight picks out the three figures supremely and it is good to stand here until the cacophony of sound or activity from elsewhere in the cathedral dies down. Even more meaningful is the experience of gazing at this scene when an orchestra, choir or organist begins a harmonious and reverent performance, for this underlines certain messages for the world.

- A world that, at creation, according to the opening words of the Bible, was formless and empty, with darkness prevailing until the Word was spoken: 'Let there be light'.[1] And that light brought order out of chaos.
- A world that was in chaos at the time of the birth of God's Son, Jesus Christ, who came to bring not just order but harmony to all who would commit their lives to him.

- A world that seems to be in chaos even today, but where there can still be harmony and order when people turn to Jesus Christ, Son of God, born into this world to show us the love of God, the heavenly Father, who sent him to die on the cross to save sinful and chaotic humanity.
- However many times this message has been heard before, it is still a world that needs to recognize it by learning to know in a better way the God who created it, letting his light shine into every corner of it.

This is the foundation on which to begin to build a better world. We often sing that the Church's one foundation is Jesus Christ her Lord,[2] but it is the essential foundation for the whole world.

When there is a restful and reverent atmosphere in the cathedral, it is the right time to return to the Epiphany Chapel to be quiet and pray.

Lord God, may the joy that comes from a trust in your power to bring order and harmony to our chaotic lives remain with us as we leave this majestic place of worship and return to our homes.

Praise belongs to you, creator God, that in the beginning you brought light to separate day and night, and saw that light as being good.

Praise to you, Father God, for sending your Son in whom was life which was the light of men and women, a light that darkness has never understood.

Praise to you, Lord Jesus, for being the light of the world, and calling people to follow you so that they need never walk in darkness, but have the light of life.

Praise to you, our risen Lord, for enduring the darkness of the suffering on the cross, then rising from death as daylight dawned that first Easter morning.

May your light ever shine before us, keeping our lives in peace and harmony.

Amen

Taking with us the atmosphere of prayer as we leave this small chapel, central in our thought is the fact that God did not simply make men and women to be in the world, but to live life to the full. As we glance again at the memorial windows, we feel the truth that he gave us nature to enjoy and artistic gifts, such as writing and music, to enable us to express our feelings. In seeking a deeper knowledge of God, we come to know ourselves better. Trying to see those selves as God's creation, our prayer must be to use how he has made us to his glory.

4

ELY

Guidebook for living

The cathedral at Ely must be one of the most visible from a distance of any Anglican cathedral in England. Standing clear against the sky in the fen country of East Anglia, it seems to beckon us. Yet, having reached the city centre, the actual approach along a narrow street is so different from what we might expect having seen it so clearly from a distance. It seems to be almost tucked away among other old buildings, yet the 215-foot (65-metre) western tower still beckons.

The main entrance is through what is called the Galilee Porch. First impressions are always significant and here at Ely ours is to gasp with delight, for this cathedral presents an open view right down its length. There is no division of the space by a screen as this was pulled down over 200 years ago. There is so much detail that could be noted, so much of interest, but our eyes are drawn along the length of the nave and upwards.

Here we have no vaulted stone ceiling, as seen in many other cathedrals. Instead, we are looking at one of wood, decorated in such a way that we cannot take our eyes from it. We are captivated by what is a colourful Victorian panelled work of art. In earlier years we would have been looking up at ugly timbers supporting the lead roof. These were boarded in during later restoration work, but this presented a great expanse of plain boarding, which did nothing to lift the spirits.

When faced with a problem, some people see it positively, as a challenge, and this is how this ceiling was seen by two Victorian amateur artists. One of them, Henry Styleman Le Strange of Norfolk, was inspired by the roof of a church in Germany and

19

so he elaborated on that as he began to paint the ceiling here. He died when he was half-way through the work, but a friend, Gambier Parry, completed it.

Their artwork comprises paintings of biblical scenes, very clearly depicting the events of both Old and New Testaments. We strain our necks to define the various incidents, identifying Adam and Eve in the Garden of Eden, Abraham and Isaac going to the place where Abraham was planning to sacrifice his son, Jacob's ladder, King David playing his harp. The sequence continues as we reach the stories of Jesus. We see Mary receiving the news that she is to have a baby and who that baby will be, and the Nativity, with the climax being the adoration of Christ. The colours, though delicate, are beautiful.

We have walked the full length of the 248-foot (75.5-metre) nave with our heads turned upwards looking at this fascinating ceiling, hardly minding how stiff our necks have become. We have missed several things *en route* as a result but, having come to what is considered to be the greatest attraction of Ely, we now concentrate on this area. The octagon and lantern tower, which surely must be unique, has been reached.

Until the early fourteenth century, there had been a square Norman tower in the centre of this cathedral, but because the pillars on which it stood were filled with rubble and rubbish, instead of being solid, it eventually collapsed. The disaster presented a challenge to the prior of Ely at the time, Alan de Walsingham, who saw it as an opportunity to create something quite new in its place. And what an amazing engineering feat this would have been more than 600 years ago. His plan was to take in the whole breadth of the cathedral, including the aisles, and create an octagon giving an area more than three times the size of the previous square on which the central tower had stood. So, the eight-sided tower, or lantern as this kind of structure is called, rose more than 140 feet (43 metres) high, with eight massive pillars supporting hundreds of tons of timber, lead and glass.

We stand beneath this towering lantern, peering up into the

centre where, according to our guidebook, there is a carved boss depicting our Lord pointing to his wounded side, but it is so high above us it is difficult to discern. On each of the eight pillars in this octagon there are sculptured corbels representing incidents in the life of St Etheldreda, who originally founded a religious house here. These carvings are, again, rather too high to see clearly.

We have no argument with those who call this octagon the glory of Ely, for it is amazing. We stand here almost in silence, just gazing, finding few words because speaking would spoil the atmosphere. There is also a modern, plain and simple altar here. This has been put in this part of the cathedral so that the celebrant is nearer to the people, and it is used for most of the services.

We pass from the octagon into the choir and are immediately attracted to the Victorian carvings above the stalls. Although they were made only about a hundred years ago by a Belgian artist, they are in keeping with the medieval carvings nearby and are beautiful. Again, biblical scenes are shown. On the south side, the carvings are of various stories from the Old Testament. Like the paintings on the roof of the nave they begin with the Genesis stories. On the north side, facing, we trace the life of Jesus from his birth to his ascension. The depiction of the crucifixion is particularly striking.

Despite the glory of the architecture here in Ely, and its fascinating history, we cannot help feeling that priority has been placed perfectly, for at the centre of this superb edifice are these representations from the Bible – the word of God. Here worshippers have this sustained reminder of the Scriptures, beginning with the story of original sin, seen in the pictures of Adam and Eve, through the dramatic events of the pre-Christian period, to the coming of the new era with Jesus Christ. Here we are reminded of the Nativity, his life of compassion, teaching and good works, culminating in his death on the cross for the sins of the world, then to his resurrection and ascension. All this is depicted here in the choir; all this is seen in the nave ceiling. Both choir and congregation, therefore, are left in no doubt as to who it is they worship and serve, and whose word must be central in their lives – that of almighty God, for the Bible is that word.

This is a salutary thought which leads us to ask ourselves, is the Bible central in our lives or does it lie on a shelf gathering dust (that is, if we even own a copy)? Perhaps we have tried to read it in the past and found it hard-going, difficult to understand. Reading one of the modern translations available can help. The amazing fact is that people have come to faith in the Lord simply by reading the Bible, so there must be something special there, something that can speak to us even in this present age. Do we feel doubtful about some of the Old Testament stories? Taken at face value, perhaps, but looking deeply there is more.

- We do not read the stories as mere accounts of what happened in history, but as having a message for today.
- The Psalms are not simply fine poetry, but superb praise to God, as well as the outpouring of every human emotion we can know. Whatever our mood when we read these ancient hymns, there can always be found something in them that seems to put our own feelings into words.
- The words of the prophets can readily be related to some present situation in our country or elsewhere in the world.
- Do we ask why Adam and Eve were evicted from the Garden of Eden? Can we see the real reason for the Israelites being led away from Egypt by Moses? Can we understand how it was a young stripling like David could overpower a giant such as Goliath?
- Do we wonder about Jonah being swallowed by a big fish (the Bible does not call it a whale!)? His prayer from the depths of the sea is meaningful, with the closing words being a message in itself, 'Salvation comes from the Lord'.[1]

We may be tempted to neglect the Old Testament, turning more eagerly to the New. It is worth remembering, however, that these old Scriptures were the ones with which Jesus grew up. In fact, he quoted from them on many occasions – including the story of Jonah! When we think about it, the whole Bible points to Jesus Christ: in the Old Testament through the prophecies, in the New Testament through revelation.

There is a significance for our visit to this cathedral in one of these Bible stories – that of Jacob dreaming about the ladder, another story Jesus referred to. Jacob's words when he woke from that dream can surely be related to the place where we are standing: 'How awesome is this place! This is none other than the house of God; this is the gate of heaven.'[2]

Indeed, something relevant can always be found in the pages of the Bible, and the more we use it, we can find it to be the ultimate guidebook for our lives. It is, in a real sense, our manual for knowing God more clearly. Through the knowledge gained by reading about him, we come to realize that he is a living God whom we can experience daily, giving us comfort in times of sorrow, peace in times of stress, conviction in times when we feel we are wrong, strength to face our problems and a challenge to make something good of our lives.

So, rather than having our lives filled with rubble, as the old pillars here were filled, knowledge gained from reading the Bible can give us that solid stability we all need. We may find ourselves fumbling about among its pages, but when we do find our way it can seem like a lantern beckoning us on, even as the tower of this cathedral beckoned us from a distance. The psalmist realized the importance of having light shining to show the way when he wrote: 'Your word is a lamp to my feet and a light for my path.'[3]

How right it is, then, that there should be this great lantern tower here where the Bible is central.

We quietly leave this part of the cathedral now for the lady chapel, which can easily be missed if we are not careful as it is set to one side of the main building. This is the largest chapel of its kind in any of the English cathedrals and very different from what we usually think of as a lady chapel. Not only is it large, but it is light and spacious. So much so that there is room for a fascinating exhibition that is displayed here at present. In each section is recorded a year in the life of Jesus, with relevant historical information given beside each picture. In this informative display, we can read how life was lived at the time when Jesus was on earth. All this adds to our knowledge of Jesus, which can encourage our living experience of him.

Lord God, we remember that at the beginning of time you spoke, and the world came into being. We praise you for calling up such a creation.

Jesus, we acknowledge that you were there at that beginning; indeed, you were the Word. We praise you for that Word becoming human for a few short years, revealing to us God, our heavenly father.

Holy Spirit, we pray you will continue to make yourself known to our hearts, speaking to our specific needs.

We ask that we may feel encouraged to find you, God, by reading the Bible and thinking deeply enough to understand the message that comes through the differing stories, the poetry, the teaching and the prophecies. Above all, we pray that we may be able to find in the Bible our guidebook for a meaningful way of living.

We are always told that the Bible is called a living book, so we pray it may become alive for us as we read it daily.

Amen

We leave the lady chapel to return to the main part of the cathedral. Walking back through the nave, inevitably our eyes are drawn again to the ceiling. If we look carefully, we can find other references to biblical stories in stained glass windows, carvings and statues. There is so much in this cathedral that is centred on the Bible. Just like the Bible, we can continue to look, to examine, to find deep truths.

5

LEICESTER

Tortured for us

Small though the cathedral in the heart of the city of Leicester is, there is such a wealth of interest here that we feel it is enormous in atmosphere and message – or, rather, messages because, although we concentrate in this visit on one theme, there are others that could occupy our minds and prayers.

Our attention is immediately arrested by a small wooden statue, covered in gold leaf, of Jesus as the good shepherd. He stands at the front of the choir gallery, shining in the sunshine that comes through the windows, a lamb in his arms. Jesus is often portrayed in this way and the thought of him leading and looking after us like a good shepherd would do is a help and comfort to us. In speaking of himself as such, however, there is more to remember, in particular his words 'I am the good shepherd. The good shepherd lays down his life for the sheep.'[1]

We know, of course, *how* he laid down his life – through crucifixion. This has become so familiar to us, but do we ever stop to remember how much suffering he went through physically, as well as the emotional and spiritual torment? It was not just the hammering of the nails through his wrists and feet and being hung up on that cross to die. Before this cruel act was carried out, there had been intolerable torture, which perhaps we sometimes tend to overlook or of which we may not know the details.

However, we are left in no doubt as to the extent of that suffering here in Leicester. Turning from the delightful little statue of Jesus as the good shepherd, our gaze is drawn upwards to the richly coloured hammerbeam roof, with its set of glorious gilded angels. Each of the angels holds an emblem of our Lord's suffering. These carvings date from the mid nineteenth century and include pincers and nails, a ladder, a seamless robe and dice, two spears crossed, one of which bears the sponge of vinegar, the cockerel and crown of thorns.

We walk down the centre aisle and into the choir, through an intricately carved screen, and stand in the sanctuary in front of the high altar and reredos, which is a memorial to the dead of World War I. The magnificent stained glass window above the memorial is part of it and illustrates the 'hope for a better new world'. Christ is seen surrounded in the outer lights by St Martin (to whom this cathedral is dedicated), St George, St Michael and St Joan of Arc. The window is a symbol of 'the power that rules the universe and the hope for peace', a leaflet tells us.

Turning to our left, we pause to look into St Katharine's Chapel, with its carved panel behind the altar showing Jesus on the cross with his mother Mary on one side and his disciple John on the other side. Then we continue into the north transept.

Here we find, almost tucked away in a corner, something that startles us and grips at our hearts. It is a seventeenth-century painting of Italian origin entitled *The Scourging of Christ*. The suffering on Jesus' face is deep and marked, even though as yet there is no crown of thorns on his head. This scourging was part of the torture meted out to prisoners in those days. Often we have read the familiar words 'Pilate took Jesus and had him flogged'.[2] We try to think of what was entailed in that flogging, or scourging. What did the body of Jesus actually endure during that time of torture?

- We realize that Jesus would have been stripped of his clothing and his hands tied to a post above his head. One thing that can be said about the Pharisees is that they would try to ensure the law was strictly kept by insisting that no more than 40 lashes be given, but we wonder if the Romans made any attempt to observe this Jewish law.
- With horror we think of those lashes being given with a

whip consisting of several heavy leather thongs, each having two small balls of lead attached near the end.

- We cringe as we think of that heavy whip being brought down with full force again and again across the back of Jesus, his shoulders and legs.

- Already Jesus had been battered and bruised from being struck across the face when he was questioned by the high priest. By now he was dehydrated and exhausted from a sleepless night, being dragged across Jerusalem from high priest to Pilate, then to Herod and afterwards back to Pilate.

- Now, suffering more bruising, his skin torn to shreds and bleeding extensively, the exhaustion had intensified so much that it is almost unbelievable he was still alive. Many had been known to die under such torture. Jesus must have been an extremely physically fit man.

- And it was on that torn, bleeding, battered back and shoulders that they placed the heavy, rough beam of the cross.

Glancing back at those angels high up on the roof of the nave, holding those symbols of his suffering, we remember Jesus' words to Peter in the Garden of Gethsemane when he tried to defend Jesus with a sword. 'Do you think I cannot call on my Father, and he will at once put at my disposal more than twelve legions of angels?'[3] Yes, of course he could have done so, but he did not. Accepting his humanity, he limited himself to that status, steadfastly accepting all the suffering a man would endure at the hands of enemies. Then the sobering thought comes, that he let it happen to him for us, for you and for me, to take the full weight of our wrongdoings on himself so that we do not have to experience the punishment they should bring.

We move back to stand in front of that great stained glass window above the high altar, realizing how linked it is with our thoughts. For it was because of his sufferings that he is now raised to glory, and because of that suffering he has the right to rule over us, controlling our lives, bringing us hope for a better world. His is the power needed to rule not only ourselves but the universe. His is our only hope for peace.

We turn and silently walk back down the central aisle, then, as we get near the good shepherd statue, Jesus' words, following on from his thoughts on the good shepherd, come clearly to our minds: 'I have come that they may have life, and have it to the full.'⁴ Yes, that was why he laid down his life for us, his sheep, that was why he endured all the suffering of the torture and crucifixion, the humiliation, loneliness of the cross, spiritual torment. It was so that we might have life and have it to the full, knowing the sins of our humanity could and would be forgiven, when we repent, because he had borne the punishment for us. Thoughts of him as the supreme good shepherd lead us to know him more clearly.

> *Heavenly Father, how you must love the world to allow your Son, Jesus Christ, to endure the suffering we should know because we have not lived as you intended when we were born. Humbly, we thank you.*
>
> *Lord Jesus, our hearts overflow with emotion, but we simply want to express our gratitude that you willingly, for love of us, accepted your role as prophesied in the Scriptures of the suffering servant, smitten and afflicted, pierced and crushed for us so that, by your wounds, we might be healed because, like lost sheep, we had gone astray.⁵ We marvel at your willingness to fulfil all that prophecy, to offer your back to those who beat you, and that you did not hide your face from the mocking and spitting.*
>
> *Lord, we are amazed that you allowed yourself to be led like a lamb to the slaughter. Surely you did take up our infirmities and carried our sorrows. So, when we suffer for any reason, you are one with us. Having looked into your suffering more deeply, we feel reassured that you understand ours.*
>
> *We are ashamed that, too often, we still go astray. But we praise you that still you come after us, looking for the sheep that goes off on its own instead of keeping close to you and staying within the flock.*
>
> *For all your sufferings, and for all they mean, we give you thanks. Amen*

Before leaving the cathedral by the Vaughan Porch, we look at the windows in the south aisle, each one showing an appearance of Jesus after his resurrection. We are particularly taken with the depiction of Jesus' meeting with Simon Peter on the shores of Galilee, when that disciple was completely assured of forgiveness for his denial and reinstated as the leader of the disciples. If ever a man knew what new life meant, it must have been Simon Peter. He went on to live it to the full by serving his Lord, winning thousands to faith in him. He himself – according to legend as well as indications in the Bible – was no stranger to suffering but he kept true to Jesus right to the end.

6

BLACKBURN

King of kings

At the heart of Blackburn Cathedral, over the altar, hangs a symbol of what is at the heart of our Christian faith – the sufferings of Christ. It is not, however, the usual crucifix, but a 'corona', representing the crown of thorns that the soldiers, in their jesting, pressed down on the head of Jesus at the time of his trial. It is a symbol that is clearly seen immediately on entering this light, airy and spacious cathedral.

The sanctuary has been sited at the crossing, so that when there is a large congregation everyone can see the service from wherever they happen to be seated and the altar is square, so it looks the same from each side. Here, standing near the altar and looking up at that meaningful corona, we can look above and beyond the corona to the rood screen. It shows Jesus on the cross with his mother on one side and the well-loved disciple, John, on the other. Above our heads, we can see a symbolic boss on the ceiling of the lantern tower. Behind a dove representing God's Holy Spirit, there are nails and a cross – a further reminder of the suffering endured by God's Son.

Looking back at the corona, the enormous wrought iron circle has spikes sticking out all round. We cannot help but wince as we think of that crown, plaited by the soldiers from branches of an acacia-type bush with thorns inches long, and how Jesus was mocked and called 'King of the Jews'.[1]

Yet, he had all the marks of kingship during his life. He was a different kind of king from that desired by the Jews, it is true, but a man with regal dignity, particularly throughout that last week of his earthly life.

- On the first Palm Sunday, the people had shouted in praise, 'Blessed is he who comes in the name of the Lord . . . the King of Israel.'[2] Later, the disciples remembered how a prophet had written, 'See, your King is coming, seated on a donkey's colt.' And the animal he chose indicated that he came as the King of Peace, not a war lord, who would have ridden a horse.

- A few days later, he demonstrated that he had come as a Servant King. We remember how, at the Last Supper, he took a towel and a basin and went around the circle of his followers, washing the dirt from their feet.

- Sadly, the praises of the people were not to last, or maybe it was a different crowd who, within a few hours of that meal, were shouting, 'Crucify him'. That was when the soldiers, hearing the Jewish leaders saying Jesus claimed to be a king, decided to have some fun with him and made the crown of thorns, playing a game they often played with prisoners called, 'The game of the king'. The game depicted a Suffering King, but the wounds from the thorns pressed on his brow would have been nothing compared with the deep emotional wounds the jesting would have caused. He would have longed to be their king, but they were simply playing a game.

- Pilate did, of course, try to save Jesus from crucifixion, asking the people, 'Shall I crucify your king?' The people, though, rejected him as king: 'Take him away . . . crucify him . . . we have no king but Caesar.'[3] Caesar! The very Roman leader they despised, the leader of the nation that occupied their country. Caesar – not Jesus – as king. Jesus was a rejected king.

- The notice Pilate put above Jesus' head on the cross stated quite clearly, 'The king of the Jews.'[4] Yet it was not just as king of the Jews that he died, but as king of us all, for he was the King of Salvation. This was his greatest service to humankind, to die that our sins could be forgiven. When he is accepted as King of Salvation, we experience him as a Forgiving King; even more as a Loving King.

As we draw near to the altar, our eyes still fixed on that corona, we see something more. Crystals are dotted among the spikes, suggesting jewels. They have been put there to remind us of the royal diadem now worn by our risen and ascended Lord. He reigns as King in heaven, but wants also to reign in our hearts. A verse from the New Testament comes to mind: 'We see Jesus, who was made a little lower than the angels, now crowned with glory and honour because he suffered death, so that by the grace of God he might taste death for everyone.'[5] That thought alone makes us want to crown him as king of our lives.

The corona is powerful and moving, but there is something in this cathedral that speaks even more to our everyday living. We turn to look back down the nave at a remarkable statue above the door by which we will eventually leave the cathedral. Again, it is made from wrought iron, and is known as The Worker Christ. The figure shows Jesus with the large hands of an ordinary working man, but they have the marks of the nails in them, reminding us of his greatest work. He wears a worker's apron and, instead of a halo, wrought iron strands above and behind the figure indicate the tradition of weaving in Lancashire, with its background of warp and weft of woven cloth. The thought coming through this meaningful statue is that our Lord goes with us to our work, as we leave this place of worship, for we worship him in our work, in whatever we do, in fact, as well as in church services.

In the far corner of the north transept, there is another most impressive statue, this one by the sculptress Josephina de Vasconcellos. It is of Mary as an ordinary mother, bathing her baby. In fact, the 'baby' looks to be almost a toddler and is anxious to get out of the bath and be busy. Mary's hand, however, holds him back and, as a result, his arms are stretched wide – a prediction of how they will be years later on the cross. Seen from the front, Mary's expression is one of a happy mother, but the expression looks different when viewed from the sides. From the left it is one of adoration, while from the right we see sorrow. Mary's boy Jesus must have seemed to her king of her life, yet she had both joy and sadness to experience in letting him reign in her heart. We remember, too, his tremendous compassion for her as he hung on the cross.

There is no lady chapel as such in this cathedral because its special dedication is to St Mary the Virgin. The chapel at the east end, behind the sanctuary, is therefore called the Jesus Chapel and, as no service is taking place at present, we sit there quietly, thinking of Jesus, our king. He is seen here in a special icon behind the altar showing him at the moment of resurrection. Interesting details include his burial shroud and bandages, while on the canopy over the altar can be seen, again, the crown of thorns and the nails of his suffering. We spend some time here praying to our risen king.

Jesus, our king, when you were here in the flesh, the only crown you were given was made of thorns, and men pressed it down hard on your brow. And you let them – why? How you longed that they should repent of their wrong thinking and be forgiven their evil minds. Help us, too, to repent of impure, unkind and deceitful thoughts.

No royal sceptre was given to you to hold, only nails driven into your hands to hold you to a cross. And you allowed it – why? Because of your love, so people would realize how deadly were their actions and be forgiven. Forgive us when our hands lead us into wrongdoing and hurtful deeds.

No dais was set up for you to mount that you might sit on a royal throne. Instead, your feet were nailed to a cross of wood and, with you fixed to that cross, men raised it up and jolted it into position. And you did not prevent them – why? Praying instead for their forgiveness, that they might understand what they were doing. Forgive us, too, when we insist on going our own way, turning our backs on you rather than continuing to walk with you.

To make sure of your death, the soldiers finally thrust a sword into your side and pierced your heart. Why should God allow this cruelty? We know it was because he loved the world so much he wanted to bring total forgiveness to everyone, including us.

Jesus, king you are, and king you will ever be, yet what we most want is that you will be king in our ordinary, everyday working lives, reigning in everything we do.
Amen

As we leave this cathedral and look up at The Worker Christ, we take with us the joy of the thought that he goes with us into our everyday working lives. As we experience him there, we realize we will know him more clearly.

7

TRURO

Is it nothing to you?

We have been told to look for two particular works of art in Truro Cathedral, both on the north side. We therefore pause only briefly when we enter, appreciating the particularly pronounced loftiness of this, the first Anglican cathedral to be built on a new site in England since the thirteenth century. Although it is traditional in style, it is only a little over 100 years old. The architect, John Loughborough Pearson, described as a man of deep Christian conviction, declared that his aim was 'to think what will bring people soonest to their knees'. That aim is achieved as we study the first of the works of art to which we have been directed.

We have walked down the nave aisle as far as the crossing and central tower, turned to our left and into the north choir aisle, and find that other visitors are grouped in front of a terracotta panel, just quietly standing there looking at it. Entitled the Via Crucis, it is by George Tinworth and shows a crowded scene of people accompanying Jesus as he makes his way to Calvary. He has just been relieved of carrying the heavy wooden beam for the cross, the Roman soldiers having compelled Simon of Cyrene to carry it for him after Jesus had stumbled and fallen.

There are dozens of figures carved into the panel and the facial expressions are remarkable, every one an individual. Those expressions leave us in no doubt as to what each person is thinking. In the centre Jesus stands, having just lifted himself up from the ground, raising a hand in a loving gesture towards his friends in the crowd.

- We see the distressed women, those Jesus calls 'Daughters of Jerusalem', as he tells them not to weep for him.[1] We detect St Veronica among them, ready to wipe his face with the cloth that has now become so precious.
- We see contempt and smugness, even a hint of triumph, on the faces of the Pharisees.
- In the foreground are the two thieves who are to be crucified with him, and the difference in their expressions is most striking. There is a harsh scowl on the face of the unrepentant man, and deep remorse on that of his companion who is turning away.
- The Roman soldiers mostly show indifference. After all, this was all in a day's work for them, even though it might be distasteful to some. We remember, however, how the centurion later acknowledged, 'Surely this was a righteous man'[2] as he watched him die. By then some of those apathetic soldiers would have been in possession of Jesus' clothing, having cast lots for it.
- Not far from Jesus we see Simon of Cyrene begrudgingly lifting the heavy wooden cross, although in his face we can see the beginnings of a softened attitude as he looks into the eyes of Jesus.
- Away at the left side of the panel stands a quite different couple, who must represent Pilate and his wife. There is the shadow of guilt on Pilate's face, but still that obstinacy. His wife looks grim and slightly frightened.

Words from Wensley and Maunder's well-known sacred cantata 'Olivet to Calvary' say it all: 'The Saviour King goes forth to die! . . . On, on to Calvary's fateful hill, Reviled by those He came to bless; But in His suffering bearing still, the majesty of Righteousness!'[3] And as our eyes scan those figures, we cannot help wondering what our faces would have shown had we been there.

An Old Testament prophecy has often been related to Jesus. We have no record of him uttering the words, but we feel we want to put them into his mouth: 'Is it nothing to you, all you who pass by? Look around and see. Is any suffering like my suffering?'[4]

You may have walked the route Jesus took in Jerusalem, known there as the Via Dolorosa, trodden the narrow streets, cobbled underfoot, arched overhead, shops and market stalls selling fruit and sweetmeats either side. It would have been a similar scene that first Good Friday — people going about their ordinary daily business of buying and selling, curious perhaps about the tragic procession of 'criminals' going to their death, but used to such sights and unconcerned. Among them, though, would have been some of his true followers and how many of them remembered his words, 'If anyone would come after me, he must deny himself and take up his cross and follow me'[5] and, '. . . anyone who does not take his cross and follow me is not worthy of me'?[6] Had he meant that they, too, were to die this way by following him? Not necessarily so, of course, for there are other ways in which we 'take up the cross'.

We now move away from this poignant treasure of the cathedral and go into the north transept, where we find a reminder of many who can be counted as worthy because they followed Jesus in a sacrificial manner. The foundations of Christianity in Cornwall were laid by the Celtic missionary saints of the fifth and sixth centuries. This soon becomes evident in travelling around the county because many of its villages and towns are named after saints, names like St Anthony, St Clement, St Dennis, St Goran, St Ives, St Just and many others, most of whom we know little if anything about.

The saints of Cornwall are delightfully commemorated in a fascinating painting here in the north transept, which was unveiled by the Prince of Wales in 1980, the centenary of the laying of the foundation stones of this cathedral. Painted by John Miller, and known as 'Cornubia — Land of the Saints' it shows an outline of the aerial view of Cornwall, the location of each church within the county marked with a Celtic cross. Away in the distance comes a long procession of Celtic saints, arriving with the light of Christ, and a shaft of light beams down from the head of the procession on to the cathedral itself.

We notice how history is acknowledged to a tremendous extent here, for in the stained glass windows either side of the nave are portrayed Christians of the ages, including Joan of Arc, Cranmer, the Venerable Bede, Edward the Confessor, Edward White Benson, who was the first bishop of Truro and, near the south-west corner, John Wesley, who had such a tremendous influence on Cornish Christianity. All these denied themselves, took up their crosses and followed their Lord. As they grew to know him more clearly, such was their response.

With thoughts of that last walk Jesus made as a man on this earth, and the saints that followed him sacrificially, we move into a quieter part of the cathedral known as St Mary's aisle or, as the locals call it, the 'church within a church'. When the cathedral was built in the nineteenth century, much of the old St Mary's parish church on the site was demolished, but, at the architect's insistence, this aisle was left standing. It is, in fact, still used as the parish church for the city centre. Truro cathedral, therefore, has a parish church, as it were, tucked into its side.

There is a seventeenth-century organ in St Mary's aisle and, as we stand looking up at the attractive barrel roof of medieval woodwork, an organist is playing a hymn on this old instrument, 'We love the place, O God, wherein Thine honour dwells'.[7] Although it is so different from the main building, this little parish church within the cathedral blends in with it well. It is quiet and simple, and the beautiful window over the altar shows the Adoration of the Magi to Jesus and his mother, as well as the infant Jesus' presentation in the temple. This cathedral is indeed a place to love and in which to pray.

Lord, the story of your sufferings has become too familiar to us. Forgive us when we give it little thought.
On the other hand, sometimes we feel distressed, even as the women of Jerusalem felt, but they did not know then that resur- rection was to follow. Help us, who have experienced the joy of the

truth that you were raised from death, to remember all this means
of triumph over the power of evil to give us life everlasting.
May we know how to answer anyone who has no belief in you,
and does not even try to understand the reason for your crucifixion.
Thank you that we can serve you still, by taking up our cross and
following you even though this might make our lives difficult.
Help us to keep before us the joy you give in that service.
May our faces ever show the joy that comes from simply knowing
you and growing daily in that knowledge of all you endured in
your human form.
Amen

Emerging from St Mary's aisle, we come back into the cathedral
proper, into the south aisle, passing what is considered to be the
oldest thing in this place. It is the fourteenth-century Breton
Pietà – the crucified Jesus being received into the arms of his
grieving mother, Mary. The cathedral is dedicated to her and we
remember how she herself followed her son right to the foot of
the cross, and experienced his love and compassion as he died.
Just three days later, how great must have been her joy when her
son, who had been born of her in an ordinary earthly manner,
rose from death in that unique and divine way.

8

ST ALBANS
The man who is God

The cathedral and abbey church of St Alban is special – for everyone, because it is on the site of the place where the first British martyr met his death, and for me personally, because I lived and worked within the sound of its bells for three years. During that time, whenever I felt overwhelmed by the pressures and problems of my work, I would try to find a half hour or so to walk quietly through the cathedral. This never failed to calm my spirits as I gained a sense of perspective. Indeed, as soon as we walk into this magnificent house of God, the vastness of the structure, coupled with the extensive history of the place, brings deep peace.

The place of pilgrimage here is, of course, the shrine of St Alban, situated behind the high altar in a secluded chapel. We will reach the shrine later.

Alban was a citizen of Verulamium, the Roman city in this area at the time. During either the third or fourth century (thoughts vary about the exact date), he received and sheltered in his house a persecuted Christian priest, usually named as Amphibalus. Alban was so impressed by the priest's prayers and piety that he asked him about the faith and soon accepted it and became a Christian himself. When the Roman authorities discovered where the priest was hiding, Alban changed clothes with those of his visitor, enabling him to escape. The Romans arrested Alban, then dressed in the priest's distinctive cloak. When the deception was eventually discovered, his witness was memorable: 'I worship and adore the true and living God who created all things.' He was subsequently condemned to death and beheaded on a hillside outside the Roman city.

In the course of time, pilgrims came to the site and a church was built that had a monastic structure. It was later rebuilt by the Normans, using the building materials from what by then had become the old deserted Roman city.

All this, and more, we find depicted in a recent addition to the cathedral walls, just inside the main entrance on the north side of the nave. Here is a 14-yard (13-metre) fabric collage that was sewn and assembled in 1992 by 450 children from about half-a-dozen schools working in groups. The collage is, in effect, a thumbnail sketch of the early history of the abbey, long before it became a cathedral.

During our visit there are, in fact, several groups of school-children being shown around by their teachers, and it is notice-able how quiet and reverent they are as they look and listen.

Having traced the early history of this place from the collage, we go from the nave, completely divided from the choir and presbytery by the nave altar and rood screen, round to the spacious crossing with its 100-foot (30-metre) tower and the transepts. The ceilings are gloriously painted here.

In the north transept we come to an altar dedicated to the 'Persecuted Church', which links the persecution of Alban with the victims of modern oppression. Ministers from several different denominations either participate or are present at the regular services here, and prayers are said for various parts of the world where Christians are, even in this day, being persecuted.

We turn from this area and stand in front of the high altar with its glorious screen. Central in it, as we would expect, is the crucifix. This brings to mind an inscription that used to be on one of the massive pillars in the nave, but has now been moved: 'I am on the cross for thee. Thou that sinnest cease for me. Cease . . . I pardon. Fight . . . I help. Conquer . . . I crown.' The figure of Jesus on the cross is surrounded by those of angels, saints and historical characters. It is all magnificent, but there is something else here that particularly holds our attention.

Beneath the crucifix is a row of 13 smaller figures, represent-ing the apostles (Judas has been replaced by Matthias) and the Saviour. And beneath that is a bas-relief sculpture, the subject of which is the resurrection. We see the figure of Christ rising from the tomb and, over his head, the hands of God hold his crown of thorns. Two angels, one on either side, have removed the cross and the earth – symbols of his burdens. The figures are made of marble and the iridescent angels' wings of paua shells from New Zealand.

Surely there is more than the resurrection shown in this exquisite panel. Yes, Jesus would have felt the relief of having that crown of thorns lifted from his head and of knowing that the intense suffering of the cross was over. But would he have accepted that the burdens of the world were left behind? As well as the resurrection, there is the message of ascension here, reminding us that, although received back into glory by his heavenly Father to be seated at his right hand, he took with him not only his earthly name, 'Jesus', with all that meant of salvation, but also his manhood. As such, the work he did in his human form is still being done by him in heaven, for Scripture tells us '. . . he is able to save completely those who come to God through him, because he always lives to intercede for them'.[1]

- When we are not able to understand the Scriptures, or the Christian way, he gives us insight.
- When we cannot decide the way ahead, he gives us guidance.
- When we find it difficult to pray, he hears the throbbing of our hearts.
- When we feel unclean because of things we have done wrong or what we have been through, he brings a sense of forgiveness and reconciliation with God.
- When we become depressed because all around us seems to be in turmoil and we cannot find peace, he reminds us of the good news that he cared so much, he died to save the world.
- When we worry about our health, he gives his touch of healing deep within our hearts.
- When we grieve over the loss of a loved one, he brings us comfort.

- When we are overwhelmed by the pressures of daily living, he says, 'Come to me . . . and I will give you rest'.[2] This text is carved on the sculpture either side, 'Come unto me . . . all ye that labour'.

It is because he became a human, lived on this earth in an ordinary family, laboured as an ordinary man and died as every human must die that he understands completely what we go through and can therefore pray for us in the presence of God, our heavenly Father. This deep truth may seem unbelievable and we feel the mystery of it, but, when we reach out to him in prayer ourselves, we know the absolute certainty of it. Jesus represents us before God and continues for ever to intercede for us, able to do so because he knows what it means to be human and can therefore plead our cause. In the panel, the hands of God lift the crown of thorns from his head, an angel carries away the cross, but although another angel holds the world, the weight of that world's burdens are still felt by him. Still his heart aches because of the suffering of the world.

We walk away from the high altar, into the quiet chapel of St Alban. This shrine has always attracted pilgrims seeking spiritual and physical healing, and the peace felt within it certainly has a calming effect. No one seems to speak here; people just stand silently and reflect on the life of a man who, although only knowing the Lord for a short time, was willing to do as he had done – give his life to save another. We feel sure Alban would have found the strength to stand firm because he knew Jesus was interceding for him in heaven.

Turning from this small chapel, we pass on into the lady chapel where we can sit and pray.

Lord, our praise and thanks to you that when you rose from death, you did not leave behind all the experience of living a human life, but did, in fact, 'take to heaven a human brow'.[3] Our thanks continue as we realize it was, and still is, because of your love that you are willing at all times to plead our cause before the heavenly Father.

43

We know you understand why we live our lives the way we do, why we go wrong, the influences that lead to our making mistakes. Forgive us, we pray, when we do not listen to your still small voice telling us what we should do.

When we are perplexed and overwhelmed, may we remember to ask ourselves what you would do in the circumstances and, however difficult that may seem, follow in your way.

As we think more deeply about your earthly life, and, by so doing, grow to know you more clearly, may this make a vital difference to our own lives.

We claim the power of your Holy Spirit, left here to help us in all these ways.

Amen

A lunchtime service is just about to begin in this lady chapel, so we stay to participate, going to the altar rail to receive bread and wine and, in so doing, experience again the meaning of that death on the cross. The last few words of The Alban Prayer (available in the form of a small card from the bookstall) are those to take with us as we leave this cathedral: '. . . Christ, who is alive and reigns, now and evermore.'

PART II

To love thee more dearly

9

NORWICH

Jesus lifted high

The cathedral at Norwich is supposed to have been built as a penance by its founder, Herbert de Losinga, several years after the Norman conquest. That being so, he certainly made up for what was considered to be his sinfulness, that of being involved in a simony scandal (paying for appointment to a high church office), for the result is one of the most magnificent of our cathedral buildings. His real character is recorded to have been holy and generous.

The colours of the magnificent west window shine as the early spring sunshine streams in and we are gripped and held not only by their brilliance, but by the clarity of the window's message. After even a short time of contemplation, that message is obvious.

Although the window was constructed in the fifteenth century, the glass in it is Victorian and there are six pictures. The three lower ones are from the life of Moses, and the three above them show relevant links with Jesus Christ. The idea of this design is that each can help us to understand the other. To the left, we see the scene in which the baby Moses is found among the rushes in the river by Pharaoh's daughter, and above is the Nativity scene of Jesus. On the right side of the window, Moses stands holding the tablets on which are inscribed the Ten Commandments, while above, Jesus sits teaching the Sermon on the Mount. In the centre, Moses is holding up the serpent in the wilderness and, above, is the glorious figure of the ascended Christ.

We stand enthralled by this comparison of the great figure

47

from the Old Testament who told the children of Israel that God would raise up a prophet like himself from among them. The one who was so raised up we now know, of course, was infinitely greater and was himself lifted up. We remember the verse that tells us, 'As Moses lifted up the snake in the desert, so the Son of Man must be lifted up'.[1] Because of that, Jesus looked ahead and prophesied, 'I, when I am lifted up from the earth, will draw all men to myself'; and the comment by the Gospel's writer was that he said this to show the kind of death he was going to die.[2]

We ponder on the link between the Old Testament story and that of Jesus being lifted up on the cross to die. We remember how Moses led the Israelites away from captivity in Egypt, but how they seemed to find plenty to grumble about in their wilderness wanderings, until God allowed a plague of venomous snakes to attack them. Then they really had something to complain about and soon realized their sin in speaking against the Lord and against Moses, praying that the snakes would be taken away. So, on God's instructions, Moses made a bronze image of a snake, put it on a pole and held it high. Then, anyone who was bitten could look at that bronze snake, remember God and find healing by trusting in him.

So, we ask ourselves, what is the connection between that rather strange story and Jesus dying on the cross? Simply that, when we look up at the cross with Jesus dying on it, we can find healing and forgiveness, because his death there was for reconciliation with God. Yet, it is not Jesus on the cross we see portrayed above the picture of Moses holding up the snake in the desert, but Jesus in glory. He is only in glory, though, because of the cross. Was this the reason for his suffering, that he might be received back to glory? There was so much more to it than that. It was because of his unique love that he let himself be so lifted up. That, if nothing else, is what leads us to love him more dearly. Significantly, all through this cathedral we find references to Jesus being lifted up on that cross.

We turn from the window and take a view right through the

nave with its lierne vaulted ceiling, an earlier and different design from the more usual fan vaulting we often see in old buildings. Here, the short stone ribs 'tie', as it were, the longer ones together. And it is at the joints of those ribs that we see richly carved and colourful bosses. We are told that there are well over a thousand of these bosses on the ceilings of this cathedral.

So lofty is this nave vault that we find it difficult to distinguish with the naked eye what the bosses show, but moveable magnifying mirrors help and both Old and New Testament stories can be picked out. Beginning at the tower end, they illustrate the Old Testament from creation to King Solomon, then the New Testament comes into view from the birth of Christ to the Last Judgement, finishing at the west end. And here, yes, we see Jesus being crucified. Later, as we walk around the quiet cloisters, we are able to see the bosses there more clearly as the ceiling is lower and here again Jesus is shown lifted up on the cross.

In fact, we lose count of the number of places in which we do see this scene. As well as in the bosses, we are reminded of the crucifixion in nearly every small chapel, of which there are at least half a dozen.

We have been given a leaflet at the information desk entitled, 'A Faith Tour of Norwich Cathedral', in which it is commented that visiting a cathedral can be 'a kind of pilgrimage or voyage of discovery'. We decide to follow the route around the small chapels as indicated in the leaflet. At each stopping place, a subject for prayer is suggested and we use each one as we progress on our tour to remember how Jesus spoke from the cross.

- Behind a glass door at the far end of the south transept is St Catherine's Chapel, where we pray for all who suffer persecution and martyrdom today. We remember how Jesus prayed, saying 'Father, forgive them, for they do not know what they are doing'.[3]
- Retracing our steps and turning right into the ambulatory, we soon reach the Bauchon Chapel, with its delightful

modern statue of Mary, the mother of Jesus. Here it is suggested that we pray for our nearest and dearest, and for family life in our country. We remember how Jesus thought of his mother and committed her to the care of his disciple John by saying, 'Dear woman, here is your son'.[4] At the cross, that mother's soul was pierced, as foretold by old Simeon when Mary and Joseph had taken the baby Jesus to the temple. A meaningful painting of this incident also hangs in this chapel.

- Continuing, we reach St Luke's Chapel, where we sit and meditate on a wonderful fourteenth-century painted reredos, where again we see the crucifixion depicted. It can also be seen carved on the font here. It seems quite natural to pray for the sick in this chapel, as St Luke was a physician. We remember, too, how Jesus spoke to the dying and penitent thief, assuring him he would be in paradise with him that day – surely words of deep healing.

- At the east end, we come to St Saviour's Chapel, which nowadays is the chapel of the Royal Norfolk Regiment. As we remember the words of Jesus 'I thirst',[5] we feel sure that was not merely a physical thirst (although it would have been great), but one of intense longing for people who fight, or even just quarrel among themselves, to turn to him and become calm and refreshed.

- In the Jesus Chapel, events of his early life are shown in paintings and windows, reminding us of his humanity. It is suggested we pray here for God's blessing on our work, but remembering also the unemployed, the hungry, the homeless and the destitute. This is so appropriate as we remember how Jesus was especially concerned for those in such distress. He worked hard himself, but, as he hung on the cross, his greatest work was accomplished and he cried with a shout of triumph, 'It is finished'.[6]

- We now go round to the north transept to look into St Andrew's Chapel, where it is asked that our prayers be for those who try to spread the gospel both at home and overseas. This is especially comforting for the many in the Third World who are overwhelmed with hunger or sickness and feel forsaken. We hear the echo of Jesus' tormented cry, 'My God, my God, why have you forsaken me?'[7] The message of the gospel taken to these people is that God does not forsake them, and that Jesus is right there with them in their suffering.

- We decide to return to the first of these chapels and, on our way, pass a candle stand and intercessions board. There are so many people for whom we want to pray and perhaps we feel a little helpless as we think of the world's needs, but here we remember how Jesus finally prayed, 'Father, into your hands I commit my spirit'.[8] We, too, can place all our deep concerns into the hands of our God, knowing he hears our prayers and that, because we have prayed, power is released for them to be answered in his way.

So we are back at St Catherine's Chapel. This place is now a gem. For 300 years it was used just as a vestry, but in 1988 it was restored as a place for silence and quiet prayer. It is small and quite plain, except for the altar, on which stands a glass cross. As we go close to the cross, we are surprised to see, instead of Jesus there, the influence of the serpent, for there are several engraved in the glass. This is so appropriate for, remembering the early Genesis story about the serpent tempting Eve in the Garden of Eden, we naturally associate snakes with evil, and it was to break the power of evil that Jesus died on the cross and rose again. There he fought the battle of good against evil, nailing evil to the cross for ever. He gained the victory of good over evil, a victory over death. In those moments when we feel overwhelmed by evil and death, we can raise our eyes to the cross and experience our deliverance.

Lord, it is so difficult to express our gratitude to you for allowing yourself to be lifted up on the cross for the sins of the world, and therefore for our sins. We recognize that this was an act of amazing love, and we can only respond by loving you in return.

Forgive us, Lord, that too often we keep our thankfulness to ourselves, neglecting to lift you up because of the way we live, failing to witness to your love and convey that love to others.
Jesus, we have thought about your words spoken from the cross, and we pray we may have the same kind of spirit within us. Help us to be more ready to forgive and, therefore, to find forgiveness.
We place into your hands, Lord God, our prayers for healing, for family and friends, for people who do not know you, for those who suffer unjustly and who feel forsaken, knowing you will hear and answer them in the best interests of all.
Amen

As we quietly leave this special place, our hearts echo a couple of lines from a well-known crucifixion hymn: 'Love so amazing, so divine, demands my soul, my life, my all.'[9] Jesus' death on the cross has drawn people to him in their millions, from every nation on earth, over the intervening centuries. And it has done so purely and simply because of his love.

It is a love that calls for a response, and it comes in the words of the saintly lady forever associated with this city, St Julian. She is shown kneeling in prayer in another beautiful window in the Bauchon Chapel. In the words from her famous fourteenth-century book *Revelations of Divine Love*, 'The one thing that matters is that we always say Yes to God whenever we experience him.'

Yes, that is all he asks. We do not have to do anything as a penance – as the founder of this cathedral felt he must – we simply have to acknowledge him as Lord.

10

LICHFIELD

All have sinned

There are children everywhere around Lichfield Cathedral during the schools' summer term. As we approach this stately building from a narrow street, the three graceful spires, known as the 'ladies of the vale', beckon us. As we get nearer, we become aware of the schoolchildren gathered in great numbers on the green outside the cathedral, eating their picnic lunches. They are here in connection with the annual Open Day project sponsored by the Lichfield Diocesan Board of Education.

The aim of the project is to give the young people an opportunity to explore and reflect on the Christian way by spending a day in the cathedral, interrelating with adult Christians and children from other schools, areas and cultures. This event has been taking place for the past 20 years. Each day for two weeks, nearly 200 children, aged between 9 and 12, come with their teachers to enjoy a tour of the cathedral, be introduced to the organ, share thoughts and feelings, enjoy activity workshops, as well as making what is called a medieval pilgrimage. The day ends with worship.

All these things we get glimpses of during the time we spend here, making this particular cathedral visit something rather special. It has to be good education to introduce youngsters to a great house of God and help them to understand not only the history behind it, but the reason for its existence. Taking groups of children on visits to our cathedrals is something that is increasingly evident, and the reverence the youngsters show in these buildings is notable.

The presence of such large numbers of children does mean,

of course, that we are hindered and cannot examine in detail some of the areas we would like to. The floor of Lichfield's extensive nave is sensibly covered with plastic sheeting for this period, and small tables have been set up at the sides with groups of children gathered around them involved in various crafts. The limitations of the visit are, however, a small price to pay for being able to observe the keen interest and tremendous enjoyment of both young people and the accompanying adults, as well as the volunteers on duty in the cathedral who are here to add to the information being given.

We have been told to be sure to look at a special sculpture at the eastern end of the south choir aisle and a volunteer guide tells us the story behind it. We therefore make our way there and are entranced by its beauty. The clear white monument is called The Sleeping Children. Here lie two sisters, Ellen-Jane and Marianne, daughters of a cathedral prebendary, who died early in the nineteenth century. Apparently the older girl died first of a serious illness, and the younger one was so distressed by her death, and so traumatized by being without her, that later she also died. They are shown, therefore, lovingly entwined in each other's arms.

We may be tempted to feel a shade sceptical at the apparent purity of the picture the memorial presents, but the sculptor, Sir Francis Chantrey, was realistic. He has gone on record as saying that no one is perfect except God himself, so he made it a habit always to carve an imperfection into his work. The guide has suggested where to find the flaw in this particular sculpture. Running our fingers along the foot of one of the girls, we feel a pronounced lump beneath the toes.

From this spot, we can look across to the north choir aisle where there is a monument to Bishop Ryder, also carved by Sir Francis Chantrey in pure white stone, but there seem to be differing ideas about what the imperfection in that statue is – a missing heel or missing ring?

It is, however, the beauty of these sisters that grips us, and we feel it is so fitting that a lovely floral arrangement has been placed beside the sculpture, adding to the feeling that, despite the built-in imperfection, there is almost unblemished beauty here. Yet, those sisters, so obviously devoted to each other, would of course have been anything but perfect when they were alive, being just ordinary children. Likewise, the bishop, kneeling in sculpted form across the cathedral, would have known within himself how imperfect he was, for he, too, was only human.

As we stand here looking at the two young girls, we are aware of the bustle of today's lively children around us. Most of them are moving about reasonably reverently and quietly, but some are becoming a little boisterous and are having to be restrained. Yet, a place of worship should be a place where children can be themselves as nearly as possible as they find the spiritual side of their nature.

The sculptor knew the truth about human nature. He understood that – as Scripture underlines – all of us have sinned and fallen 'short of the glory of God'.[1] Nowadays, many of us do not like the word 'sin', especially if we consider ourselves to be pretty good people, not doing anyone any harm, helping where we can, living clean lives, giving to charity. But just what is sin? We do not have to look far in today's world to find crime. Perhaps we feel we would never commit the kind of acts of violence we see and hear about daily on the media. Too often, though, we get bogged down with what is or is not a sin and forget the true definition, that sin is simply ignoring God and going our own way. All those other things we call sin, such as lying, stealing, murder, worry, immorality, unkindness and so on, are essentially the results of sin, the effect of living our lives apart from God.

- When we remember that at creation God made men and women good, we can realize how far short we have all fallen of the glorious ideal he set for us.
- We know we do fall short, we miss the mark of that ideal, as seen in his son Jesus Christ. We all do it – either as a result of weakness, carelessness, lack of understanding or because of the circumstances of our lives.

- Because of our experiences, we may be aware of certain iniquities, indicating a somewhat bent or crooked attitude to life that results in us going astray, deviating from the straight path God intended we should walk.
- We may, however, be going along a good path, to all intents and purposes, although at the same time feeling deep inside that it is not the ideal way, not what God wants for us.
- Sin can, in fact, be summed up by the lack of love we have for Jesus. And when we treat his love for us with indifference, ignore that love to such an extent that we begin to shrug off our mistakes, to go our own way or even to deliberately turn to crime, there is a clear question that comes to us.
- The question is the same as that which Jesus asked his disciple Simon Peter after his sin of denial: 'Do you love me?'[2] When we are unsure how to answer that searching question, we do need to examine our lives for those traces of sin we may have thought did not exist.

Aware that the children are nearby, we turn into the retrochoir where they are being shown the tiles on which are depicted scenes from the life of St Chad, the first bishop of Lichfield, and the fourth of Mercia in the seventh century. Indeed, this cathedral was founded in his honour, although the original small Saxon church was later replaced by a Norman building and then, still later, by a larger Gothic cathedral. All three enshrined the bones of St Chad and each building became the focus for pilgrimages. The stories about this saintly man convey a humble, zealous person of transparent godliness. After his death, miracles are reputed to have taken place at his tomb.

Just now, one group of children, attired in sackcloth costumes and obviously in that part of the day's programme labelled a medieval pilgrimage, are kneeling on the tiles listening to the story. Another group comes to this area and stands in a circle around the ledger stone marking the place where St Chad's shrine once stood before it was destroyed during the Reformation by Henry VIII. One of the volunteer helpers leads the children in prayer, using the words of one that was connected with St Chad. We catch some of the words, that we may, like him, '. . . be inspired to devote ourselves wholly to Thy service; and ever to maintain the virtue of love and of peace one with another . . .' Most of the children are very reverent, seeming to listen and hopefully praying, although one girl is looking around and obviously not hearing a word. No, there is never perfection, even in what at first glance seems to be a group of perfectly behaved children!

We return to the south choir aisle and retrace our steps until we come to a narrow flight of steps that we go up and find ourselves in a tiny and peaceful place of prayer. This is St Chad's Head Chapel. The volunteer guide tells us that morning prayer is said here daily by the dean and cathedral canons. The chapel is empty at present as the volunteer is waiting for some of the children, so that he can show them a plaster skull of the saint and talk about him. In earlier centuries, the skull of St Chad was covered with gold leaf and kept here to be exhibited from the gallery to passing pilgrims. We sit here quietly for a time, glad that this small chapel has been set aside for prayer.

Father God, we bow before you, humbly acknowledging that, as all other human beings, we too have sinned. Indeed, we are daily sinning, forgetting you, ignoring the love you have for us, going our own way, perhaps straying a long way off the straight path or even turning to crime.

Our prayer is that you will forgive the sins we commit, forgive even those of us who should know better. If we have been unaware of sin, make it known to us in such a way that we may willingly turn from it and try, with your help, to make our lives closer to how you would have us live.

As we acknowledge that we are not perfect, we are just human, we feel warmed as we experience your great love enveloping us, reassuring us and giving us the comfort and blessing of your forgiveness. For this we thank you, heavenly Father.

Yet, even as we are bowed before you, even as we feel the warmth of that love, we are conscious of two things your son Jesus would say to us. We hear his question, 'Do you love me?'² and respond,

as did his disciple of long ago, 'Lord, you know all things; you know that I love you.'
And then we hear that command he gave to those who were repentant, 'Go, and sin no more'.[3] Heavenly Father, give us the strength that we may carry out that command.
We thank you now that, having received your forgiveness and been assured again of your unique love, we do not need to keep a sense of guilt, but may go on our way not only determined to avoid sinning, but rejoicing in all you mean to us.
Amen

Returning to the ground floor, we see that the children have been ushered into the exquisite lady chapel for worship. We have been told that when St Chad 'came to Lichfield, he brought Christianity to the centre of England' and surely his work continues, with the cathedral not only keeping alive Christianity here, but encouraging it in future generations. As we leave, those members of a future generation are singing heartily some modern-day worship songs.

11

MANCHESTER
Joy in heaven

There are angels in Manchester Cathedral, plenty of them. More than a dozen are playing musical instruments in the nave, while ten more support emblems in the Regiment Chapel. Oldest of all is the Angel Stone, on view on the north side of the chancel arch.

We feel in need of a guiding angel before we reach this cathedral for it is not easy to find, enclosed as it is by a sea of traffic-jammed streets, and overshadowed by high-rise buildings. Indeed, its 130-foot (39-metre) tower is not visible until we are nearly beside it. Once found, however, it is magnificent in a traditional kind of way.

Entering on a dull day, it looks a rather gloomy and forbidding place, so it seems natural for us to immediately turn to our left and make for a brilliant window we can just glimpse at the far end on the north side. Here we step into the Regiment Chapel, our eyes fixed on the blazing red of the window behind the altar. This is known as the Fire Window and represents the devastation of the war-time air raid that severely damaged a great deal of this cathedral in 1940. Some parts have never been rebuilt, but this chapel has and the restoration has been superb. There are no lights on at present, but the window adds a warm glow to the chapel, although it does not brighten it enough for us to be able to clearly see the carvings of angels on the new roof.

As we sit here, peering up at them, a member of the clergy comes in and, as we begin talking with him, he tells us that when the sun is shining through the window in the early morning, the whole chapel is aglow, a wonderful sight. He then obligingly switches on the lights and there are the angels in full view. Five pairs of them are in flight over our heads, each pair supporting a different emblem.

Angels have several different roles in the Bible, and our experience in this chapel reminds us of words of Jesus when, speaking about children, he said that 'their angels in heaven always see the face of my Father'.[1] Angels are mysterious creatures. Indeed, we do not really understand much about them, but we can be sure that, although we do not normally see them, they are there in the shadows, keeping watch over the Lord's people.

The Bible gives several instances, both in the Old and the New Testaments, where these unseen protectors are working, appearing to the human eye only when necessary for reassurance or challenge. Likewise, in modern times, people have had unusual experiences that they can only attribute to some invisible force at work in their situation. There are war-time stories as well as personal adventures. Even though we may not ourselves have had such experiences, they are very real to some people and we cannot deny them.

We leave this chapel and make our way round behind the choir and high altar to the lady chapel. The chapel was rebuilt to a new design after that devastating air raid, although the sixteenth-century screen was undamaged and remains. The walls have been brightened by the addition of some interesting tapestries woven in the late 1950s portraying scenes from the Annunciation and the Nativity. The tapestries show those stories so clearly that inevitably we remember another role of angels in the Bible – that of messengers.

- From Genesis right through to the opening of the New Testament, God sends his angelic messengers to certain people to convey what he is about to do.
- The Christmas stories in Luke's Gospel are full of angels. Gabriel's appearance to the Virgin Mary troubled her greatly, but she believed and accepted the message he brought.
- The angel appearing to Zechariah the priest, at the side of

the altar, giving him the message that he and his wife Elizabeth would have a son (John the Baptist), was a frightening experience. Zechariah did not believe, so was struck dumb until the birth of his boy.

- The shepherds in Bethlehem's fields received the most glorious message from the angel that a saviour had been born, followed by the great company of heavenly beings praising God and saying, 'Glory to God in the highest, and on earth peace to men on whom his favour rests'.[2] Their immediate response was to take action and go to see if they had dreamt it or if the vision had been true.

- Throughout his Passion, we know that Jesus was conscious not so much of angels as messengers, but of their power. In the Garden of Gethsemane, when he prayed in such anguish, there was an angel from heaven with him, strengthening him.

- When Peter tried to defend Jesus in that same garden, he was told to put away his sword. Jesus said he could, if he wished, call on twelve legions of angels to come to his rescue. He did not do so, however, knowing the only way to save the world was to die for it. Yet we can be sure those legions of angels would have been keeping watch over him in his battle against evil.

- Later, Peter was to experience the intervention of an angel, helping him to escape from prison. However we interpret such a story, we can be sure God was behind that rescue, answering the prayers of the Church.

We may not experience heavenly beings nowadays in these ways, but still God sends his messengers to speak to us and help us. We may be seated in a church service, listening to a sermon, a Bible reading or singing a hymn, and the words seem to hit home in such a way that we cannot forget them. Is this not God speaking through his messengers of preacher, reader or writer?

In our personal battle against wrong in our lives, we can be sure of God's unique help to overcome it. Sometimes, indeed very often, this help comes via a friend, and our response is an involuntary exclamation, 'You are an angel!' We have to simply submit ourselves to the Lord and he will send his angel of help.

We return to the front of the chancel arch and eventually find the Angel Stone, which is much smaller than we had thought it would be. This stone is but a small fragment of a Saxon church, probably the first to be built on this site, dating back to the eighth century. It shows an angel bearing a scroll. The Saxon words on it translate as 'Into thy hands, O Lord, I commend my spirit'[3] – words spoken by Jesus from the cross.

Turning from the Angel Stone, we next look high above to the nave roof where, because the lighting is on, we can see clearly a heavenly orchestra, as well as sculptured bosses representing the sun shining in splendour surrounded by clouds. The dark wood and stone do tend to give this cathedral a sombre feel, but wide clerestory windows, camber beam roof and graceful pillars help the atmosphere. The roof is supported by seven huge beams of moulded oak and it is at the top of the wall posts supporting them on either side that we see the musical angels, each one playing a different fifteenth-century instrument. They are so high above our heads that they are not absolutely clear, but, according to the guidebook, they are playing the harp, trumpet, recorder, tabor, Irish bagpipe, Scottish bagpipe, shawm, clavicymbal, portative organ, psaltery, dulcimer, lute, fiddle and hurdy-gurdy. Having read this list, we fix our gaze upwards and they do gradually seem clearer, so that it takes just a little imagination to hear the music coming from them. Here, it seems, is the main role of the angels – to praise God.

The last of the psalms in the Bible seems to be illustrated by this heavenly group. Some of the same instruments are mentioned and, more importantly, the reason for the angels making music. It is to 'Praise the Lord', to 'Praise God in his sanctuary; praise him in his mighty heavens . . . for his acts of power . . . his surpassing greatness'.[4] But is this the sole purpose for angels making music? Praising God with the clash of cymbals and the delightful sounds of other instruments is a great thought, but there is another reason for their rejoicing. Jesus told us about it when he said, '. . . there is rejoicing in the presence of the angels of God over one sinner who repents'.[5]

The trumpets and cymbals may well herald one such sinner into Christian faith. It could be a really startling experience that has brought this, something to shout about. And we hear many stories of people coming to faith this way. There are, however, quieter instruments – the harp, other stringed instruments and the flute. For many people, the quiet influence of a Christian friend, their upbringing in a Christian home or the example of a saint of today may have gently led them, first to a knowledge of God, then on to a deep love for him because of the way he sent Jesus into the world to live and die among us. Both kinds of experience can blend together in the way an orchestra harmonizes. The binding force is simply a love for the Lord, a love that grows more dearly each day. When that happens, there really is joy among the angels in heaven.

We walk across to the Jesus Chapel in the south aisle. This is a place of tranquillity. Hanging above the altar is an impressive and unusual cross, with an intricate woven design. There is no service taking place here just now, so we are free to sit quietly and pray.

Mighty God, we praise you for the thought of your unseen heavenly host, ever keeping watch over this world, and over each one of us. We thank you for the strength this thought brings.

Lord, help us to be alert to the messages you send us through human 'angels', so we may discern when they are words from yourself that we need to take notice of.

Heavenly Father, in times of danger, or when we are faced with difficult situations or even tragedies, reassure us that we can always call on you to send us the strength and guidance we need, by whatever means. Above all, may we add to the rejoicing among your angels as we come to you in repentance.

Make us know that your angels in the heights do help us to adore you, almighty and everlasting king of heaven, God of grace.

Amen

As we leave the Jesus Chapel, we step back down the aisle and take a look at the entrance to the chapter house. The mural paintings in the tracery above the door illustrate the beatitudes and the Sermon on the Mount. We remember how Jesus said in that sermon that we should let our light shine so that our good deeds would cause people to praise our heavenly Father.

The memory of those angels, hidden in the shadows but always there singing and praising God, lingers, and we know we will find strength to let our own light shine.

12

COVENTRY

Father, forgive

Many people have two fixed ideas about Coventry Cathedral before visiting it: one, that the modern part of the cathedral will not appeal, and the other that the message to be found here will be centred on 'forgiveness'. The first idea is completely turned on its head as soon as we enter the new part of the cathedral. The other thought is confirmed and, indeed, emphasized. The two ideas, we discover, are interlinked here because the appeal of the new building has much to do with the fact that everything has been designed to symbolize forgiveness and reconciliation.

The obvious place to begin our visit is in the old part of the cathedral. People throughout the world know the scene well. The bombed ruin, tidied up, of course, but still open to the sky. The focal point here is the Altar of Reconciliation, on which stands the cross made of two of the charred medieval roof timbers that fell across each other in the air raid of November 1940 and were discovered the following morning amid the rubble. They were tied together, set up in the ruined sanctuary and have stood there ever since. After that night of horror, how imaginative and utterly Christ-like to have the words, 'Father, forgive' inscribed behind that charred cross.

At that same time, a local priest created another cross by binding together three of the large medieval nails that were strewn among the other debris, thus creating the Cross of Nails that has become the symbol of Coventry's international ministry of reconciliation. We will come to this cross later in our visit as it is set within the high altar cross.

65

These were the kinds of acts that led those involved with Coventry Cathedral at the time of the air raid to confirm within themselves the faith of the gospel story of death and resurrection. The resolve to rebuild the cathedral was born on the morning following that raid; the thought of new life coming just a few hours after such destruction is deeply moving.

Visitors crowd to this ruined part of the cathedral, and at dawn on Easter Day and Whit Sunday Holy Communion is celebrated here. Today the crowds are swelled by several groups of schoolchildren. Our prayer should be that they may be encouraged to think about the message of forgiveness and reconciliation so powerfully conveyed here.

Standing in front of that charred cross, at present by ourselves for a few moments, we remain almost silent, reading the words, 'Father, forgive', remembering how they were spoken by Jesus as he was nailed to the cross, dying to save the world. We only begin to understand the message of forgiveness when we think of that cross, for Jesus did not merely teach us to forgive, he gave us the supreme example by showing forgiveness himself.

As the nails were driven into his hands and feet, he prayed, 'Father, forgive them, for they do not know what they are doing.'[1] Who was it he was praying for?

- Father, forgive the Roman soldiers who are nailing me to this cross. They do not know what they are doing – they think they are merely carrying out their orders, not killing the Son of God.
- Father, forgive Pilate, he did not recognize he was looking truth in the face.
- Father, forgive the Pharisees, they shut their eyes to the fact that they had condemned the very Messiah they were looking for.
- Father, forgive the thief dying on the cross beside me who is not repentant. Forgive his curses – he does not know who is dying with him.
- Father, forgive Judas, he did not understand what he was doing by betraying me.

- Father, forgive Peter – he did not realize how he was deny-
ing me.
- Father, forgive the disciples – they did not think they were
letting me down by forsaking me and running away.

And looking ahead into the future, he was praying for friends
and enemies alike, praying for all who would sin.

- Father, forgive those who fight against each other, even
when they say they are doing so in a holy war – they do
not understand the way of peace.
- Father, forgive those enemies of Britain who bombed this
great place of worship – they only knew they must obey
orders or suffer at the hands of their leaders.
- Father, forgive my Church, supposed to be the body of
believers, forgive their quarrelling and divisions – they do
not see how they are harming the witness to your love.
- Father, forgive the writer of this meditation, and those who
read it – we do not stop to think, we do not realize how we
can hurt by carelessness, by lack of concern, by resentment.

God not only listened to the prayer of Jesus from the cross, he
granted it, for forgiveness was, and still is, offered to all who in
turn learn how to forgive others.

It has been so right to begin our visit here, in the place where
wartime evil created such devastation, for it is here, experiencing forgiveness ourselves, we know we too can begin afresh.

There is only one way to go after accepting that forgiveness
and that is towards new life. So we pass from the old to the new,
realizing we are not visiting two cathedrals but one, although in
two parts. Walking from the bombed ruins into the new building is like proceeding from Good Friday to Easter, from death
to new life. The thought of human cruelty is left behind as our
attention is completely drawn to and held by the enormous and
superb tapestry at the far end, beyond the high altar, of Christ in
Glory.

Indeed, the glory of Christ fills this new part of the cathedral, a glory made meaningful because of that unique act of

forgiveness. We are more aware of this glory because everything here speaks of him, without the encumbrance of other monuments. The tapestry so dominates the scene from almost every angle that the eyes of the Lord appear to follow us and a sense of his presence pervades. Those eyes and his presence seem to be asking silently, 'Having received my forgiveness, are you too willing to forgive other people?'

As we pass the font, placed in front of a brilliant stained glass window, and remember that this rough, three-ton boulder was brought from a hillside near Bethlehem, we wonder, did those words of forgiveness include Herod's terrible killing of innocent babies at the time of the birth of Jesus?

We pause in the south aisle in front of a rather unusual crucifix, a gift from Czechoslovakia. Instead of Christ being portrayed hanging on the cross, an image we are accustomed to seeing, his body has been carved into it, thereby becoming part of the cross. It prompts the thought that Jesus is the cross.

One small chapel that seems to speak more than almost anything else here is the Chapel of Christ in Gethsemane with its surround of a wrought iron crown of thorns, through which is seen the mosaic called the Angel of Agony. In the angel's hand is a cup, which reminds us of Jesus' prayer in the Garden of Gethsemane, that he might not have to drink this cup of suffering. He added, though, '. . . yet not my will, but yours be done'.[2]

We reach the lady chapel where we are right up close to the tremendous tapestry, able to see the wounds in Christ's hands and feet. Between the nail-pierced feet stands the figure of a human being. That is where we, too, want to be – at his feet, worshipping Christ in glory, who died that we might know complete forgiveness and reconciliation with our heavenly Father.

Lord, as we humbly bow before you, we are filled with thanksgiving that your love led you to die for us so we could know forgiveness for all we have done wrong, all the ways in which we have not met your standard of holiness, all our mistakes.

Those wrongs, failings and mistakes that we sometimes feel we can never forgive ourselves for, we just now bring to you, laying them at your feet.

That forgiveness we sometimes find difficult to accept, we just now open our hearts to receive with gratitude.

The sins you know are in our hearts which we sometimes find hard to put away, just now we feel the strength you give us to overcome.

We think of the lack of forgiveness in our hearts for other people, often the hardest thing we have to cope with, just now we think of what you said on the cross, then feel confident enough to pray, 'Father, forgive us our trespasses as we forgive those who trespass against us.'

May the peace of reconciliation fill our hearts.

Amen

After noting how the original Cross of Nails is set within the high altar cross, we walk back down the nave on the north side. An impressive sculpture near the entrance to the Chapel of Unity takes our eye and sends us away with the memory of Jesus' forgiving spirit. Simply entitled Christ Crucified, it shows the head of Christ wearing the crown of thorns, his eyes closed as if in prayer. The work of Helen Jennings, it was created from a wrecked motor car. As Coventry is the city of the motor car, this is so apt.

Carrying with us the knowledge of the forgiveness shown by our Lord as he was crucified, and feeling the deep love he has for us, he could not have done anything more to move us to love him more dearly.

13

ROCHESTER

The ups and downs of life

Although Rochester has the second oldest cathedral foundation in England, it only shows its age in a few places. Otherwise it feels as alive today as it ever was.

We find one evidence of its age at an old doorway on the north side. The door stands open, allowing us to peer through into the depths of some of the early crumbling foundations. Rochester's first cathedral was established early in the seventh century, but because of Danish raids and other disturbances it was destroyed more than once and nothing of the original Saxon edifice can now be readily seen.

Through this ancient doorway, too, there is a short passage leading to Gundulf's Tower, and it is the name of Bishop Gundulf that is associated with the rebuilding that took place soon after the Norman Conquest. It is on record that this Norman bishop, although small in stature, was renowned for his piety, leadership and effectiveness as a builder. He also helped to establish a Benedictine monastery here. The door is marked 'Private', so we do not venture further, but we understand that the tower is now used for choir practice.

Nearby is a flight of steps known as the Pilgrims' steps. The stone steps themselves have been covered with wood to preserve them. We ascend these steps, which thousands of pilgrims would have used as they visited the shrine of William of Perth. On a pilgrimage himself, William was murdered and his body brought into the cathedral where healing miracles were said to occur at his tomb.

This cathedral has seen more than its fair share of disruption

70

during its long history. King John plundered it in his time and later even more damage was done by the troops of Simon de Montfort. Fires, ravages by iconoclasts at the time of the Reformation and during the Civil War and Oliver Cromwell's seventeenth-century Commonwealth, as well as war damage in the more recent past have all contributed to its life story, leaving it with a somewhat gnarled appearance. For all that, there is a pleasurable atmosphere about it, similar to the kind of feeling experienced when in the company of a very old saintly person who, although wrinkled, has the peace and joy of the Lord shining from within their heart.

How fitting is the message of a mural we see as we come to the north-east side of the choir. Entitled Wheel of Fortune, it is part of a thirteenth-century wall painting, which was hidden behind a pulpit until its rediscovery in 1840. The inscription tells us that it was cleaned just a few years ago and is one of the finest medieval wall paintings in the country. A wall tablet further enlightens us, pointing out that it portrays the 'ups and downs of life' but 'only the figures showing man's ascent remain'.

How we would love to have seen the complete painting, but what we can see is fascinating. There is a clear wheel motif still in view in which the figures are set. This idea of life being a cycle is not unique, of course, for the natives of North America have legends based on this same thought. They say that the circle represents the cycle of life in that all life travels in a circular path.

The whole cathedral seems to echo this thought. There would have been great days of rejoicing as building was started and eventually completed, followed by despair as invaders and vandals ruined the work, leaving behind devastation. High hopes felt as new Christian leaders came to this place, among them men like John Fisher and Nicholas Ridley, both early sixteenth-century bishops of Rochester, would have been followed by despair as each, in his turn, was martyred. What sadness people would have known when damage was sustained during World

War II. Then what rejoicing towards the end of the twentieth century as pilgrims were welcomed here for a service in remembrance of the 1400th anniversary of St Augustine coming to this part of England.

We glance along the line of choir stalls beside this meaningful mural, behind which we see painting of a different kind. The pattern is of fleur-de-lis and leopards, and it is claimed that every leopard's face is different, representing the many faces of humanity. There are too many leopards to count or verify that they are, indeed, all different, but the thought comes that even as every human face differs, so every human has his or her own 'ups and downs of life' and none of these is the same.

We turn, now, to stand in front of the high altar, studying the small reredos there. This is not magnificent, but very appealing. The carved stone figures make up the scene around the table at the Last Supper. Most of the front has been left empty so we can see Jesus handing the bread and the wine to his disciples. At each end of the table is a disciple, while the others are ranged behind it. We feel we want to step into that scene, standing at the front of that table, to take and eat the bread, to drink the wine in remembrance of the day our Lord's body was given and his blood shed for us. A pair of candles and the altar cross rather obstruct our view. Yet, we think, the cross stood before Jesus in his mind as he handed his followers the bread and wine.

We leave this part of the cathedral and go into the lady chapel to be quiet for a while. This chapel is unusually situated at the angle of the nave and the south transept, instead of at the east end, because originally there were monastic buildings located there in this cathedral. The chapel is light and spacious with some beautiful windows. From the arranged seats we can look towards scenes of the Nativity, but, turning, we can see the crucifixion as well as the ascension.

In his humanity, Jesus knew all about the ups and downs of life. As we sometimes sing in one of our Christmas carols, 'Tears and smiles like us he knew.'[1]

- At the time of his birth, the angels in heaven rejoiced, humble shepherds came to visit him and wealthy wise men presented him with costly gifts. Simeon and Anna in the temple praised God because of him. Yet, within a short space of time, Herod sent out his soldiers to try to find and kill him, but was unsuccessful because Joseph and Mary had fled with him to Egypt.
- When the family was eventually able to return to Nazareth and set up home there, it must have been a happy place, with Jesus having brothers and sisters with whom to play and grow up. In his many parables, we get a glimpse of the kind of home they had and much of it seems to speak of a pleasant life.
- Later, however, when we realize that Joseph had died, Jesus would have become bread-winner for the family, assuming the role of village carpenter. It would not have been easy for him, especially as he would then have been looking ahead to fulfilling his real purpose in coming into the world.
- The time did come, of course, for him to leave his home and his first public appearance was when he was baptized by his relative, John the Baptist. What a tremendous day that must have been, as he distinctly heard God, his heavenly Father, confirming his role and stating his pleasure in him.
- The 'down' side came immediately afterwards, when Jesus went into the desert to ponder on the way in which to conduct his mission. It was during this time of decision that he was sorely tempted to undertake the work he had come to do in the ways of the Devil.
- As we read the gospel stories, there are many 'ups and downs'. How great must have been his joy as he called those first disciples and they followed him so readily. How glad he must have felt to have been able to bring healing and peace of mind to the many people who flocked to him for help. How pleased when the crowds sat or stood before him drinking in his every word as he taught.
- Then again, how distressed he must have been when some

of the Jewish leaders misinterpreted his words and deeds. How angry he felt at their hypocrisy, their lack of compassion and their obvious jealousy.

- What hurt would have been his when some of his followers turned their backs on him because they could not stomach some of his difficult teaching. Yet, how relieved and glad, by contrast, he would have felt when his close circle of friends remained loyal, recognizing he had the words of eternal life.

- What a joy for him to have the friendship of people like Mary, Martha and Lazarus, and to know he was always welcome in their home.

- What a disappointment for him when people like the rich young ruler turned away because the cost of following him was too great.

- How difficult for him to leave behind Galilee, with its beautiful countryside and peaceful atmosphere, and make his way to Jerusalem, with its busy and crowded streets, and the hatred of the Pharisees and scribes.

- How he would have loved that last meal with his close followers, giving his final teaching, serving them. Yet, what sorrow, too, filled him as he silently appealed to Judas Iscariot to consider what he was planning to do.

- As they went into the Garden of Gethsemane, how he would have felt the comfort of the three closest to him. Yet, what sorrow there was when he found that they had fallen asleep instead of keeping watch, sorrow that would deepen when they all ran away as he was arrested.

- Perhaps as he hung on the cross there would have been some comfort in looking down and seeing his mother and one disciple standing there. Yet, surely this was also the lowest point in all history and the worst suffering that could be known.

- It was not to be the end. As that early mural shows people on the ascent, there is always the point of rising when we trust ourselves into the hands of our God, as Jesus did.

Our prayer is that we may love our Lord more dearly. We cannot help but love him when we consider how he chose to leave his riches in glory and come to earth to live the ups and downs of human life with us, and more. Appropriately, a prayer card from the information desk suggests that we pray for the Holy Spirit to 'lead us to journey deeper into the mystery' of his love.

Leaving the lady chapel, we go down a flight of stone steps quite near to it and find ourselves in the crypt. This whole area is large and interesting, but it is the crypt chapel in particular that draws us. Here is a place in which we can be completely still and quietly pray.

Lord Jesus, we thank you that you were willing to come to earth to live an ordinary human existence, knowing its pleasures as well as its sorrows and, because of that, you understand us so perfectly. We are glad that you did know joy as people came to you, listened to your teaching and followed you, showing their love for you, but we are sad that some were harsh, unkind and then eventually so cruel.

Yet, Lord, as we remember the different reactions of people when you moved about among them, we acknowledge that we sometimes ebb and flow in our feelings towards you, and for that we want to ask your forgiveness.

Even as people long ago turned from you when they found your teaching hard, we are sometimes tempted to turn away when things do not go the way we want them to, and for that we repent.

Lord, give us strength to keep loyal to you at all times, trusting you fully, knowing that you love us perfectly even though our love for you sometimes grows cold.

Show us how we can help to raise the spirits of other people who are going through a low patch, to enable them to feel your love.

Amen

We climb the steps from the crypt, coming back into the main part of the building, but then up a further flight of steps to the south choir aisle to look at another old doorway. This is the chapter room doorway. Beautiful, intricate stone carvings surround its arch.

High up on the wall nearby is a memorial to Charles Dickens, for this was the town in which he lived and wrote. This nineteenth-century novelist knew much about the 'ups and downs of life' and drew people's attention to the plight of the poor and destitute when he wrote about them. He surely offers a challenge to those of us who bear the name Christian to do what we can to ease the burdens of people who know too much about the 'downs' of life and not enough about the 'ups'.

14

CARLISLE

Meekness and majesty

Carlisle has a cathedral without a real nave. The greater part of it was knocked down at the time of Oliver Cromwell, its bricks used for building the city walls, and it was never fully restored. What is left of the nave has now mainly become the Border Regiment Chapel. The entrance to the cathedral is therefore by the south door in the south west transept, so we walk immediately into the crossing and turn our attention to what is the main part of the cathedral, the choir, where daily worship takes place.

The opening in the choir screen is narrow and we cannot see in advance what is beyond. The shortened nave and unusual placing of the main entrance do not prepare us for the beauty we now see. Our immediate reaction as we enter the choir is to exclaim with pleasure and surprise on looking up at the ceiling as it is wonderfully painted in bright blue and liberally sprinkled with golden stars. The sight prompts just one word, 'majesty', and we stand beneath the ceiling silently worshipping the majesty of the Lord we serve. Here is grandeur and dignity befitting the king of kings.

This feeling increases as we look towards the high altar, which is dominated by the east window. The top tracery of the window is medieval and depicts the Last Judgement. The lower part is Victorian glass and the scenes it shows bring a second word to our minds, 'meekness', for pictured here are events from the earthly life of Christ, the central one being his crucifixion. These remind us that he did in fact lay aside his majesty and come to earth as an ordinary human being. Above the crucifixion

77

scene in the central panel is the ascended Lord, so linking the two thoughts we often sing about these days, meekness and majesty.

It seems appropriate, therefore, that scenes from human life should be depicted in the stone capitals at the tops of the pillars around the presbytery and choir. There are 12 in all, six either side, and each one is different. Together they illustrate activities that would have been undertaken by a medieval farmer, and are known as the Labours of the Month.

The carvings are not too easy to see, being high up and not that large, but it is well worth straining our necks to find them and try to see what the farmer is doing in each month of the year. Particularly amusing is the second one in from the altar on the south side. This is February, when a man sits in front of a fire, warming his toes and pouring water from his boot. Next is March, where he is seen pruning his vines, and on the opposite side, across the choir stalls, is September where he is shown gathering the grapes. The first in the series shows a man with two faces, the symbol of the god Janus for January.

The thought of the majesty Jesus had with his Father in heaven, coupled with the reminder of the meekness with which he came to earth, is a sure prompt for our love to grow more dearly. We recall the ordinary kind of life he lived, by the standards of the day, and his wholehearted interest in everyday affairs – it all comes out in the parables he told.

- Jesus lived in an ordinary family home and saw how different siblings were from each other, perhaps becoming involved in their disagreements.
- He knew the daily toil of the housewife, so he spoke about sewing on patches, using yeast in the making of bread and having to sweep the house to find a lost coin.
- Not only did he call fishermen to be his close followers, he likened the kingdom of heaven to a net used to catch all kinds of fish.
- A favourite parable was that of a shepherd so devoted to his sheep that he went after just one stray.

- He was familiar with the ways of businessmen and how, when they had to go away, they would leave their employees with certain responsibilities.
- In his younger years, working beside Joseph in the carpenter's shop, he would meet builders and learn the wisdom of building on a firm foundation, rather than the foolishness of building on sand.
- He loved nature and the countryside, speaking with affection of birds and flowers.
- He had observed the husbandry of those who grew trees, commenting on good and bad fruit.
- During his years as a carpenter, he would have made yokes for farmers to use with their oxen when ploughing. His well-loved phrase, 'My yoke is easy and my burden is light',[1] therefore carries real meaning. Perhaps he had delivered such yokes and so would see farmers plough, then sow the seeds and later harvest the crops and build barns in which to store them.
- He would have walked in marketplaces, seen merchants bargaining over pearls and other goods.
- He would know too well the imposition of the payment of taxes and the temptations that would come to those who collected them.
- He had seen the despair of those who were unemployed and stood around the marketplace day after day, hoping someone would give them work.
- He travelled throughout his own country, so understood the hazards of journeys in deserted areas.
- The main liquid intake of the day being wine, he realized the importance of vineyards and using the right kind of wineskins.

Customs may have changed, but what Jesus says still speaks to us in our daily living – in the way we care for our families, the kind of work we do, the financial concerns we have, what we do with our leisure time, how we conduct our business, the despair we know when we lose our jobs. He understands the discomfort of the farmer during the cold, wet months of the year, as well as the joys of harvest time. It is appropriate, therefore, that the capitals at the tops of the pillars in the choir convey the message of a Lord who is keenly interested and concerned about the kinds of things that we face daily each month of the year. Our God is the 'centre and soul of every sphere',[2] yet he is still nearer to each human heart than anyone else. He is majesty, but he is also meekness, sharing in our human concerns.

It is with reluctance that we leave this meaningful area of the cathedral, but we have not paid much attention to what there is in the rest of this building. So, returning to the crossing, we go nearer the north transept, which we glimpsed earlier. This is designated St Wilfred's Chapel and is used to celebrate the daily Eucharist. It contains the Brougham Triptych, a superbly carved altarpiece that shows the more spectacular incidents in Christ's life – the worship of the wise men at his birth and, in later life, Jesus carrying his cross and his crucifixion.

The window above the altar is beautiful, but there is a sad story here. It tells of five of Dean Tait's daughters, all of whom died of scarlet fever within six weeks of each other in the mid nineteenth century. Our Lord, so familiar with the joys and sorrows of family life, would have been there with the parents at that traumatic time. Their comfort may well have been that they had taught their girls to love the Lord dearly.

A kneeler is provided at the rail of this chapel, and there is a card bearing a suggested prayer that we may use or else we can pray our own prayers, as we choose.

> *Lord of our everyday, it gives us comfort to realize that, although you are high and lifted up, still you are close to us as we engage in our daily activities, whether we are working or at leisure, doing our household chores or going on a journey.*
> *Forgive us when we doubt that you will understand what we are going through and we therefore turn our backs on you.*
> *Remind us always to bring the details of our lives before you for your correction, reassurance and help. Because you have lived an*

ordinary human life, we ask that you will direct all we do, suggesting each move.

But we remember, too, that the end of your earthly life was suffering far beyond anything we can know and, because you endured
that on our behalf, we can worship your majesty as you now reign
in glory.

May our remembrance of the meekness of your life on earth and
your glory now in heaven so stimulate our love for you that our
ordinary living may be blessed.

Amen

As this cathedral is near to an area of great beauty (the Lake
District), it is fitting that, among others, there is a memorial to
the National Trust's founder, Canon Frederick Rawnsley. On the
north side of the nave is a window showing the baptism of Jesus,
not set by the river Jordan, but against the background of the
Lake District hills. As we leave, we look up at the window above
the door called The Seven Days of Creation. God, who created
a beautiful world, came to live here as a man and die to save it.

15

CHRIST CHURCH, OXFORD
Praise to the king of heaven

Tucked away among Oxford's 'dreaming spires' is that of Christ Church. Our first sight of this, one of the earliest cathedral spires in England, comes as we stand in the Tom Gate beneath the great rounded Tom Tower, which houses the seven-ton bell called Great Tom, and look across the Tom Quad.

Here is one of the oldest and smallest of England's Anglican cathedrals, although Oxford is the largest diocese in the country. Further, Christ Church is unique in that it is both a cathedral and a college chapel.

We enter at the west end from the cloisters. Our immediate feeling is of being thrilled, our spirits uplifted, so that we hardly notice any of the few other visitors or the volunteer helpers. We just stand and look down the full length of this glorious place of worship. That first impression is not, though, simply of a place of worship, but of one filled with praise. The atmosphere is almost tangible and we feel it instinctively.

The pews of the nave face inwards because the cathedral is also the college chapel. This gives a clear view right down the short nave and on into the choir and chancel to the high altar, and beyond to the rose window. The brightness of this interior is enhanced by the light honey-coloured Cotswold stone used in the building, and it is this that shows the pattern of the lierne vault of the chancel ceiling – with its 12 graceful pendants – to such advantage. The intricate star-shaped design is intended to create an image of heaven. That intention has been so fully achieved that it inspires within us music of praise.

Different styles of music seem to ring in our memory, from

'The heavens are telling the glory of God' from Haydn's *The Creation* to Henry Francis Lyte's majestic traditional hymn, 'Praise, my soul, the King of heaven; to His feet thy tribute bring.' Indeed, we want to do that – bring ourselves to the creator of heaven and earth. We think also of a more recent song by Tricia and Noel Richards, 'All heaven declares the glory of the risen Lord; who can compare with the beauty of the Lord?'

There is no need to apologize for listing these three different kinds of hymns of praise together, for surely the glory of the Lord is praised from generation to generation, whether it is in great classical music, in traditional hymns or in simple songs of praise. Each person visiting this exquisite cathedral must surely feel praise welling up in the heart, in whatever form best suits them. What a pity when there is discord rather than harmony between different tastes in music, such as we sometimes find in churches today.

- Some cannot appreciate what they call the 'happy, clappy' style of worship, perhaps feeling it is irreverent or even childish, forgetting the time when they, as young people, loved to sing choruses and join in with actions as they learned about Jesus giving them joy.
- Some find many of the older-style hymns rather tedious, lacking in that joy, not encouraging a depth of praise in their hearts for the God they worship. It may be that the words of some of those old hymns do not convey the same kinds of meanings that were originally intended, yet there are musical harmonies in some of the tunes that are good and give a feeling of reverence as well as, at times, energetic challenge.
- Nowhere is great classical music heard to more advantage than in our cathedrals as the sound echoes around the stone walls and up into the heights, giving such a glimpse of heaven that we want it to go on and on. For some, however, such sounds are bewildering and do nothing for their spirits.
- The one thought that unites us all, whatever our tastes in

music, is the reason for our making music as we worship. It is to praise almighty God, king of heaven, and his son, Jesus Christ, who died to save us. It is as our responsive love grows that our desire to praise increases.

Dislike of certain styles of praise is nothing new. We recall how the Gospels tell of the entry Jesus made into Jerusalem riding on a donkey, when people, including children, sang to him, 'Hosanna to the Son of David'.[1] The Jewish leaders, however, were indignant. Jesus' reply was to quote the Psalms: 'From the lips of children and infants you have ordained praise.'[2] It was a joy to him then, as it must be now, to hear praise from young and old alike. It did not matter to him what the style was, simply that it came from the heart.

The book of the Psalms in our Bibles is the hymn book of years ago, yet it is still relevant for us to use today. There we are told to 'Sing joyfully to the Lord' and to sing to him 'a new song'. Instruments come into the scene, too, as we are urged to 'Praise the Lord with the harp, make music to him on the ten-stringed lyre' and to 'play skilfully, and shout for joy'.[3] We are also urged to 'Praise him with . . . dancing'.[4] It is true that Christians have taken such words in a more literal way in recent years than they have for generations, but they have done so to express their innermost feelings. As they learn to love the Lord more dearly, day by day, they want to praise him with greater enthusiasm and energy than might have been the case for some time.

Thoughts about music are natural in this cathedral as it plays such an important part in its life. Throughout the week, we are told, the choir sings during termtime, and, during the holidays, many services are sung by a voluntary choir of people from the diocese. We wonder if they look up to the bottom of the tower arch where, on one side is a carving of a man playing a lute and, on the opposite, is one of a man listening!

Having walked through to the choir, we now turn to go towards the lady chapel. There are several interesting stained glass windows throughout this cathedral, and in this area we come to some of the five designed for this place by Edward Burne-Jones, who was an undergraduate at Oxford in the mid nineteenth century. One window holds our attention particularly as we have been thinking about music. It has soft colouring and, among the saints shown, is the patron saint of music, St Cecilia. It seems so right that she should be commemorated here, as music should fill this cathedral of praise. In fact, as we stand here, a soft, gentle theme is being played on the organ.

St Cecilia is listed as being one of the tutors to St Frideswide, the founder of the original convent on this site in the eighth century, and Oxford's patron saint. Her story is told in a special window to her, also by Burne-Jones, in the nearby Latin Chapel. There is a mass of detail in this window, which is quite different from the others by Burne-Jones here, but then her life was quite complicated and turbulent. She spent years fleeing from a persistent suitor and was protected from him when both he and his soldiers were struck with blindness. She was therefore free to devote her life to prayer and performing miracles. At the top of the window is a roundel showing a ship conveying her to heaven after her death. The atmosphere in this chapel, however, is peaceful, and it is the place set aside for private prayer.

With all our hearts, Lord God, we want to praise you as we learn daily to love you more dearly because of your great and mighty work and your unique love for us all.

We thank you that you accept the praise that comes not just from our lips but from our hearts. Our prayer is that you will cleanse those hearts and make them worthy to hold such praise.

Forgive us when our praise is spoiled because we are not happy with the medium being used to convey it. Help us to appreciate all styles of music that are dedicated to you.

Forgive us even more, Lord, when differences of opinion about forms of worship cause divisions within our church fellowships, so that worship becomes meaningless.

Help us to see the joy and true spirit of those who are worshipping you in a way that does not appeal to us, and help us to understand when our style does not have the same attraction for other people as it does for us.

Lord God, we do love you and we want to give you praise for Jesus, yet anything we can utter is so completely inadequate. So, we pray you will accept what our lips sing and say, and, more especially, that you will hear what our hearts yearn to but cannot fully express.

Amen

We now leave this small cathedral and make our way towards the great hall, which reminds us that we are in the midst of academic learning, among those 'dreaming spires' that house the colleges of this university city. This said, in the magnificent hall, with its array of portraits of great and learned people, is one window that holds the kind of interest that crosses the divide between the academic realm and fantasy. In it we see Charles Dodgson, better known as Lewis Carroll, who wrote the children's classic *Alice in Wonderland* while he was a mathematics tutor here. Alice Liddell, on whom he based his stories, was the daughter of the then dean, Henry Liddell. She is also commemorated in this window. Diversity seems, again, to be the exciting spirit at work in Oxford.

PART III

To follow thee more nearly

16

BURY ST EDMUNDS

The enemy's arrows

On a beautiful spring day, after the dark months of winter, it is tempting to linger in the Abbey Gardens, sitting in the sunshine near the ruins of all that remains of the great abbey of St Edmund, built by Anselm when he was the abbot here in the twelfth century. Do we really want to go indoors on such a day and look at the present building – the parish church of St James, specially built 400 years later to welcome pilgrims who came to remember a very special king?

On such a bright day, do we wish to recall the gruesome story of the horrific martyrdom of King Edmund? We resist the temptation to bask in the sunshine for the time being, however, and go into the church that became the cathedral of Suffolk in 1914. The work of transforming the parish church into a cathedral is not yet finished, but what has been done is very pleasing. We feel somewhat apprehensive that St Edmund may dominate the interior, but even though there are plenty of references to him, they are not overpowering, and his story has a deep message for us. Also, the story is just a part of the real purpose of the cathedral – a place of worship to almighty God.

We are reminded of this as soon as we enter as all the windows in this cathedral are colourful, clear and full of meaning. A great favourite, especially with children we are told, is the west window on the north side. Here we see the six days of creation, vegetation and animal life being shown as well as humans. As in other cathedrals in this part of England, we notice that a full range of biblical stories is shown in the windows, from the Old Testament on the north side and the New Testament on the

89

south, but today we are looking for the one in which St Edmund is portrayed. Eventually we find it as we approach the lady chapel. He is shown in the stained glass in what has become a traditional way, holding an arrow. Why an arrow, we wonder? A guidebook fills us in with the details.

Edmund was King of the East Angles in the ninth century. He met his death because of his Christian faith at the hands of the invading Danes, who tied him to a tree and shot at him repeatedly with arrows. Not content with that, they cut off his head and threw it into the undergrowth. Then, legend takes over where historical fact leaves off, giving us the story that his followers were guided to the severed head by a voice calling, 'Here I am'. When they followed the sound, they came face to face with a ferocious wolf who was guarding the head between its paws. The picture of the wolf with the crowned head of the king appears in the arms of this town, and the carvings on the bishop's throne here show the same scene.

The window, before which we stand thinking about this story, is quite colourful, showing a fine figure, although Edmund is not the only martyr seen here. Among the others we note a biblical one, Stephen, with people grouped around him, great stones in their hands.

We next walk through the choir to the north side and into the St Edmund Chapel, and here we find St Edmund's story depicted in a special way. In 1970, on the 1100th anniversary of his death, a pageant was enacted in the Abbey Gardens. Nine schools made banners for the occasion and these were later mounted and framed as a visual history of King Edmund's life. They now hang in sequence on the wall of this chapel, each one covering a different phase of Edmund's life. The first is of young Edmund being greeted by his uncle, who was then King of the East Angles. The second shows Edmund being crowned (we are told he ruled wisely). In the third, he is seen receiving the gift of land that was later to become Bury St Edmunds. Events in his life are shown in the other banners, the final one picturing him tied to a tree with the arrows coming at him. It is a very moving and emotional set of pictures and prompts us to feel admiration for this man who refused to renounce his Christian faith and suffered so much as a result.

As we finish looking at the last banner, we turn towards the altar. Above it is a gloriously coloured stained glass window showing not Edmund but the Lord he followed so faithfully. Christ is seen on the cross and his mother, Mary, is on one side and his disciple John is on the other. We feel sure that, had Edmund been alive and in Jerusalem at the time, he too would have stood there. We wonder if we would have been with him.

Quietly we leave the chapel, making our way up a flight of stone steps to the treasury, where we have been told there is a very special cross. This is known as the Jubilee Cross. As it is used on certain occasions in the cathedral's worship, it may not always be there, but today we can see it and a volunteer guide kindly directs us to it.

We stand, gazing at the cross, that cross which has so much meaning. The main point of interest is a crown circling its foot. It is not a crown of thorns, but a crown of arrows, recalling the way Edmund was martyred.

Nearby hangs a significant modern painting entitled Pilate Washes his Hands. The face of Pontius Pilate is shown well lit in the foreground, his hands held up with the water running over them. The figure of Jesus, with a red robe and the crown of thorns, stands in the background, surrounded by the angry mob calling for him to be crucified. We recall the incident in the gospel story of Pilate doing this and saying as he did so, 'I am innocent of this man's blood. It is your responsibility',[1] before handing Jesus over to be crucified. Pilate washed his hands of his responsibility. Edmund did not. Instead, he remained faithful.

We turn and look at a modern embroidery by a local artist hanging on the opposite wall. It shows that dreadful scene of Edmund with the arrows sticking out all around his body. The passage from the apostle Paul's writings about putting on the full armour of God comes to mind, in particular, '. . . take up the shield of faith, with which you can extinguish all the flaming arrows of the evil one'.[2] We usually think of those flaming arrows as being the darts of temptation that come to Christians. Edmund did not yield to the temptation to renounce his faith, and was willing to follow in the steps of his Lord's suffering. Jesus himself suffered temptation, just as any other human being does. And it was not only in those 40 days in the wilderness recorded in the Gospels. Throughout his life, and particularly at the time of his death, he knew the onslaught of evil lures.

- In the wilderness, as we read, he was tempted by the Devil to use his divine powers to satisfy his personal hunger, but he resisted because he accepted his humanity completely, which would not allow him to use such powers purely for his own benefit.

- As he came to the cross, he was tempted again. He was offered wine mixed with myrrh – the drugs of the day – that he might be spared some of the agony of the torture. He refused even this small comfort. If he was to die for the sins of the world, then it would be as a fully conscious man. He offered himself completely and with faculties unimpaired, determined to experience every minute, every second of pain with none of his senses dulled.

- Jesus also experienced temptation of the mind during his time in the wilderness. The Devil tempted him by interpreting the Scriptures to suit his ends, asking Jesus to put God to the test by throwing himself from the pinnacle of the temple in a spectacular show of courage and land unharmed as that would be sure to draw people to him. Again, Jesus resisted the temptation. He would not use his divinity to defy the laws of gravity. He would limit himself to what a human being would be capable of, not expecting his heavenly Father to save him from sure suicide by making such a leap.

- On the cross, a similar and deeply sinister temptation came to him, this time from the Jewish leaders who had condemned him. 'He saved others, but he can't save himself! He's the king of Israel! Let him come down now from the cross, and we will believe in him.'[3] Yes, of course he could have come down from the cross but, had he done so, would they have believed in him? Come to that, would we believe in him? Those Jewish leaders did not realize how much truth there was in what they were saying even though they were sneering. No, he could not save himself, simply because of his tremendous and unique love. He so loved the world, so wanted to save everyone within it, that he had to die for them.

- In the wilderness, there came the ultimate temptation – to reject God completely. The temptation was to sell his soul to the Devil, to go his own way, achieve notoriety by the world's standards. Then there would be no need to agonize, suffer, die in order to win people. The temptation was to use the Devil's weapons of cruelty, ruthlessness and force in a heartless thrust for universal dominion. Jesus knew, however, that evil can never be overcome by evil. The evil in the world can only be overcome by good.

- On the cross, that terrible temptation returned, as he experienced being completely cut off from God because the sin of the world had put a barrier between them. Yet, even though he cried out, 'My God, my God, why have you forsaken me?'[4] it was still to God he called. Never once did he yield to the temptation to turn against God.

We know, of course, that these temptations were not the sins he bore. Had he yielded to them that would have been so, but he resisted every last one, so he himself remained blameless, even though he carried the sins of humanity to the cross.

We do not know the full details of the life of Edmund, but we do know he did not yield to the temptation to turn his back on God, to let go of his faith in Jesus Christ, his Lord and Saviour. Jesus had died for him because he loved him. Edmund died for his Lord because he returned that love. And the truth is clear, as we absorb his story in this place, that when Jesus called people to follow him he did not promise them a comfortable life. They were to follow in his footsteps, even if that meant suffering in the way he suffered. We are reminded of the words of the apostle Paul: 'I want to know Christ and the power of his resurrection and the fellowship of sharing in his sufferings, becoming like him in his death, and so, somehow, to attain to the resurrection from the dead'.[5] Undoubtedly Edmund, sharing in his Lord's sufferings, and being like him in his death, would have attained to resurrection from that cruel death.

We leave the treasury and return to the nave as the clock strikes three, and a member of the clergy climbs into the pulpit. He reads the prayer of St Edmund, asking that we may be encouraged to vanquish every assault of the enemy. When we have echoed the 'Amen', we walk round to the oratory chapel, which is nearby, for a quiet prayer of our own. This is a small, plain and silent chapel where at present just one nun is seated praying silently. We spend some moments there for the same purpose.

Lord, for all your saints who have willingly let themselves be taken and killed because of their love for you, we humbly give you thanks and pray that we, too, may be filled with a love for you that will take us wherever you want us to go.

We acknowledge that we are tempted, even though we may each be tempted in different ways. We pray you will give us strength to resist everything that is not right for us in your eyes.

We recognize that, at such times, we are being tested. Help us, Lord, not to fail the test, because we know you will never allow us to be tempted beyond the limits of the strength you give us.

Lord, often we are tempted in our thinking. At such times, help us to rid ourselves of negative thoughts as a way of resisting that temptation. When we are tempted to worry and become anxious, give us a sense of your power.

If we are tempted to hate someone, fill us with your spirit of love. When we are tempted to repay evil with evil, teach us again that evil can only be overcome by love.

Above all, help us always to remember the truest and most assured way of resisting temptation: keeping our eyes fixed on you.

We know we may never have to suffer the way St Edmund did,

*but we pray we may always stand firm against ridicule of our faith
and opposition to your ways.*
*We do realize, Lord, that even in this modern world some of your
followers do suffer in horrific ways. We pray for all who experience
the call to follow you more nearly, that they may be given the
utmost strength to stand firm.*
Amen

We leave this small place of prayer and return to that window
showing St Edmund and the other Christian martyrs. Why do
people let themselves be killed in barbarous ways? What is it that
persuades them to put themselves into such danger when they
may simply keep quiet about their beliefs? Whatever do they
hope to gain by what is seemingly such folly? They are not the
kinds of people who would be tempted by the thought of being
known as 'saints'.

For them, this has been the way they have followed the Lord
more nearly. Not thinking of themselves, they have given those
selves completely and unstintingly to him, in sheer love and
gratitude for the love he showed everyone by dying on the cross
so that their wrongdoings might be forgiven.

17

LINCOLN

Reflecting the glory

It really needs a sunny day to visit Lincoln Cathedral in order to get the full impact of light shining through the multicoloured windows. True, anyone of average height and eyesight will find it difficult to decipher the scenes in those windows, so small are most of them and so high up are they in this lofty building, but the brilliant colours compensate, even more so when the day is bright.

The floor of the nave is usually kept free of seating except on special occasions, so the effect of sunlight through the windows decorates the floor in a surprising manner. That effect, in fact, is so startling that, having entered, we simply stand quite still, not venturing further for a few moments. Pouring down from those high windows is a multitude of colourful patterns that flow onto the floor, the surrounding walls and the clustered piers of Purbeck marble and local limestone. The reflection of those colours lifts our thoughts at once to the majesty of the Lord to such an extent that it is difficult to concentrate on other details in this cathedral, our eyes being constantly drawn back to the windows and the effect they have.

Another thought edges into our minds, one of challenge based on a New Testament verse telling us that we who 'reflect the Lord's glory, are being transformed into his likeness with ever-increasing glory, which comes from the Lord, who is the Spirit'.[1] We need to ask: do we reflect the Lord's glory, and are we being transformed into his likeness with ever-increasing glory? If we call ourselves Christians – followers of Jesus Christ – is this how we follow him more nearly?

- Do we reflect the peace he brought to distraught people?
- Is his patience seen in us, the kind of patience he showed with his disciples as they questioned him?
- Do we show kindness to people, the sort of kindness Jesus showed to the mothers who brought their children to him when he was tired?
- Does his brand of goodness shine out from us in everything we do?
- Are we faithful to those who depend on us, as he was faithful to his followers and all who sought him in a true spirit?
- Does gentleness play a part in our dealings with people, as it did when he healed, sometimes taking the afflicted person away from the glare of the public and gently giving them the help they needed?
- When people seem against us and we want to retaliate, do we exercise self-control as he did when thrust before Herod and Pontius Pilate?
- Do we have anything like the love he had for people, love that even took him to the cross to die for everyone?
- Does the joy that love brings us overflow, making us shine like lights in a dark and often unhappy world?

These are the kinds of reflections he would want to see in our lives. When they are seen in us we prove that the Holy Spirit lives within us, for these are what are known as the fruit of the Spirit, as we read in the New Testament.[2] The essential work of that Holy Spirit is to bring such attributes to fruition in our lives. When that happens, then the gifts of the Spirit so valued by Christians for the work of the Church can be properly effective.

We walk carefully through the nave, almost not liking to tread on those reflections, and into the great transept. At each end of the transept there is a magnificent rose window, and we hardly know which to look at first. They are called the 'two eyes of the cathedral' and each has its own name.

Influenced by what has been going through our thoughts, we turn first to the south-facing one, which is known as The

Bishop's Eye, so-called because the bishop looks south in order 'to receive the Holy Spirit', that Holy Spirit we need to reflect his glory. This window is fascinating, different from the usual concept of a rose window in that there is no central figure of Christ or the Virgin Mary, just fragments of medieval glass reset in the late eighteenth century amid flowing leaf-tracery.

The opposite rose window is called The Dean's Eye and this one does have the usual kind of pictures within it. This 'eye' faces north in order to protect 'against the Devil of cold and darkness', those things that hinder the Lord's reflection of glory in us. Both, surely, have their part to play in our lives if we are to follow Jesus more nearly.

We walk on into the south choir aisle and notice on one wall some striking mid fifteenth-century south German wood-carvings. There are four and they show scenes from the Lord's Passion. One is the Garden of Gethsemane, where Peter cuts off the ear of a man sent to arrest Jesus. The next one is of Jesus on the way to Calvary with St Veronica standing by, a cloth in her hand that she has just used to wipe his face. The third seems to show Jesus with the two criminals, bound together with him. In the fourth, he is being taken down from the cross, ready for burial. They are not large carvings and so are all too easily passed by, but they are very impressive. Perhaps we do not always think of those scenes as showing our Lord's glory, and yet they do, for that love must have shone out from him throughout those dark hours. Would that same spirit shine out from us if we were faced with opposition, even persecution, we wonder?

What is described as 'the heart of the cathedral' is St Hugh's Choir, which links the sanctuary with the choir to form an inner church where worship is conducted daily. It was, in fact, St Hugh of Avalon, a Carthusian monk of the twelfth century, who was largely responsible for the rebuilding of the cathedral after an earthquake. After his death, when he was canonized, pilgrimages to his shrine began, so eventually the cathedral was extended and a new choir came into being – the Angel Choir. It is so called after the 28 angels carved high up under the topmost windows. Again, it is difficult to see them clearly because of where they are, but there are two other features that hold our attention. One is the tremendous east window, showing scenes of the life, death and resurrection of Christ, and some of his miracles. Once more, the beauty is enhanced when a shaft of sunlight shoots through the glass, giving the window an extra dimension.

The other focus of attention can be seen more clearly by inserting a coin into a slot, which we do, and there, high up, is the famous Lincoln imp. It is not easy, even so, to see his horned head, crossed leg and frightening grimace in any detail, but we listen with amusement as a guide relates the legend of how the angels above him turned him to stone for misbehaving. The guide makes quite a profound comment as he ends his telling of this tale, saying 'This just shows that in the midst of so much good, there always lurks some evil.' It is, indeed, quite a thought that, even though we may try hard to reflect the glory of the Lord, being human we do fail because of the evil around us in the world, and in our nature. It is only through the power the Holy Spirit brings that we can ever hope for a measure of success. And, we wonder, can the reverse be said – that in the midst of evil there always lurks some good?

We next pass by St Hugh's head shrine (redesigned in recent years, so named because St Hugh's head was detached from his body and a shrine was built in the thirteenth century). We stand in the area of the memorial to St Gilbert of Sempringham, where huge pots stand holding candles, and where visitors can themselves light a candle and pray.

Lord, the glory we have seen reminds us of the glory that shines from you, both through your work of creation and your work in the hearts and lives of your people. We praise you that you are a great and glorious God.
We have been challenged to let your glory be reflected in the way we live as we try to follow you more nearly, but we know this is far from simple so we pray that you will send us the strength through your Holy Spirit.

We acknowledge that, even though we may feel we are living a good life, there is always at least the hint of wrong, and sometimes it is even stronger than that. Show us, we pray, how to overcome what we do not like in our lives.

Help us, too, Lord, to be able to look for and find something good in other people, even though we may feel their lives are dark, maybe even criminal.

We pray that the reflection you send into our lives may help someone else to turn to and follow you.

Amen

As we walk back to the nave, we cannot keep our eyes from those magnificently coloured windows at the east end, in the great transept and high above the nave floor. We notice that neither can one small toddler keep away from their reflection. He has left the side of his parents and is now gleefully crawling about among one set of reflections, trying to capture the colours in his hand!

Our prayer as we leave this cathedral is that young people and children may be able to see Christ's glory reflected in us and that we will be so 'transformed into his likeness with ever-increasing glory', that they will want to capture it for themselves.

18

SALISBURY

The family

Salisbury is usually crowded, especially on a warm summer day. Tourists seem drawn to this interesting city and in particular to the cathedral with its graceful spire, the tallest in England. We pass people of different nationalities as we walk across the green to the cathedral entrance, and hear several different languages being spoken.

Looking down the length of the cathedral (nearly 450 feet/137 metres), we get the impression of a unity, probably because the whole interior structure was built to the design of one man – Bishop Richard Poore – and completed without a break during the thirteenth century. We can see right through to the high altar, for there is no screen, and even beyond this to the Trinity Chapel.

We stand here at the west end for several moments, quietly admiring this great house of God, then walk on, drawn by the distant blue of the windows in that Trinity Chapel. On the way down the north side, we slip into the tiny Audley Chantry, from where we can get a close-up view of the high altar. This Chantry is a gem in itself, with a superb ceiling and an Italian painting of the Virgin Mary and baby Jesus above the small altar. As we leave it, we look up to the vaulting at the choir crossing where we can see a painting of Christ and the apostles, which is delicate in colouring and very beautiful.

It is, however, the windows of the Trinity Chapel that have drawn us on to the east end. Although relatively new (1980) the colouring is thirteenth century. This superb five-lancet window is dedicated to and called Prisoners of Conscience, and the overall impression is of blue glass. As we come nearer, however, we can see and appreciate other colours that have been used to portray the faces of many people. We are advised that we should come to look at this window more than once, in order to understand it properly. The design is what is known as 'impressionistic'. We therefore decide to move away for the time being and return later, although before doing so we look down the full length of the building from this angle and, again, there is that feeling of unity.

As we reach the crossing, three o'clock strikes and, as in many other cathedrals, this is the time for prayer; but here, although a recognized routine, it becomes something special. A member of the clergy, who we have seen walking about the cathedral, climbs into the pulpit and calls the many visitors to be still just where they are and quietly join him in prayer. We stand with bowed heads and listen to his simple and sincere prayers for the world and its needs. He concludes by suggesting that everyone says together the Lord's Prayer in whatever is their native language. We do so reverently, hearing faint murmurings from groups around us, some obviously from other countries. The short prayer-time is rounded off when he says the Grace.

The experience has emphasized for us how the prayer that Jesus taught his disciples is, in real terms, a prayer for the world. This cathedral has become what he once said of the temple, '. . . a house of prayer for all nations'.[1] And this prayer-time now becomes even more meaningful for us. Turning our heads, we realize that, as we have said this prayer together, we have been standing right beside a small chapel called the Chapel of St Margaret of Scotland, dedicated to the Mothers' Union. Two things catch our eye and leave a deep impression. One is a simple small sculpture of a mother with a child at her knee and may be meant to represent Mary and the child Jesus. The other is a framed and written thought placed in front of the chapel that says: 'As you stand here ponder for a moment the importance of family life, its joys and its sorrows. Pray that your home may be one of love and peace and joy.'

How appropriate that we have stood here, beside this chapel dedicated to the family, as we have prayed together what is often known as the 'family prayer'. Today, members from the family of nations have prayed it here together. For although we think of it as the family prayer, it is not just one to be said within the confines of our personal families, valuable as that is. Rather, it applies in the wider sense of family, our country and people throughout the world, for Jesus died not just for his own earthly family and friends, but for people in the family of nations.

This prayer is known to millions of people. It is said daily and, we have to say, perhaps without thinking too deeply about it, simply repeating the words, maybe at times almost parrot-fashion. Yet, when we think about it, if everyone who ever prayed this prayer in the 2,000 years since Jesus taught it had sincerely and wholeheartedly meant what was said, how different the world would be today. Nor is it simply a prayer to be said by ourselves alone, although it can be. It is, in the true sense, a corporate prayer, which is why we usually say it together for the words we use are 'our' or 'we' and 'us'.

- Our Father, we begin, and we remember he is Father of all. True, some members of the human race may not acknowledge him as such and others may even shrink from such a relationship, remembering cruelty and abuse from their earthly fathers, but God is all that could be wanted in a good father, and so much more. He is gracious, all-knowing, generous, reliable, welcoming, merciful, faithful, dependable, just, holy, powerful and, above all, loving.
- All these things we are saying as we address God in this way, this Father who is in heaven. For heaven does not merely indicate God's location; heaven and perfection mean the same thing.
- It is because of those wonderful attributes that we want his name to be hallowed among the nations. Those of us who know him as our heavenly Father, therefore have a responsibility to let him be known to people who may be living in fear and superstition.

103

- For that reason, we go on to pray that this heavenly Father's kingdom may come, which is really the same as praying that his will may be done on earth as it is done in heaven.
- That will includes all people. When we pray that our daily bread may be supplied, we are first acknowledging our dependence on God to provide our needs, then realizing that we have to do our part by cooperating with God by working to obtain those needs. There is, however, much more to this short phrase in the prayer than that. It underlines our responsibility to help meet the needs of other people who may be unable, for various reasons, to adequately provide for themselves. When people are starving, we know that too often the trouble is because of man's greed. It is this part of the prayer that more than any other makes it one for all nations.
- The prayer for forgiveness can, quite rightly, be taken personally but, at times, it is essential for a group, even perhaps a whole nation, to pray it together. We think of countries that have been severely treated in times of uprising or war and understand how hard it must be for them to forgive a whole nation and not just its leaders. Our example can only be Jesus, who prayed as he was being nailed to the cross that his heavenly Father would forgive everyone who was guilty.
- Temptation is very real for everyone – it is a universal experience – but however hard it is, we know it should be resisted and overcome. This is a difficult part of the prayer, but we often take it to mean that we will not be brought to the point of being tested beyond our endurance. When we pray it like that, really meaning it, our God honours our prayer.
- He does so because he alone is able to be the ultimate influence on our lives, he alone is able to deliver us from the power of the evil one, for his is the kingdom and the power and the glory for ever.
- We add the usual 'Amen' to the prayer, but we are saying far more than putting a full-stop at the end. We are saying, in

effect, 'So be it, Lord'. It is a statement that our belief is in a God who is always faithful, who will hear and answer our prayers, for he is the great 'Amen' himself. We simply have to learn how to ask in sincerity and with persistence, as Jesus taught in the Gospels.

We return to the Trinity Chapel to look again at those brilliant windows, as now we feel a prayer within us for other people, especially those who suffer for their faith. The people portrayed have different styles of head-dresses, reminding us of people from various countries. What is similar about them all is a look of anguish, for they are all suffering. Yet they are looking upwards and, being prisoners of conscience, we realize that they are looking to God for strength to overcome and win the victory over evil. Having thought through that prayer for the family of nations, we feel the responsibility to pray for those who suffer, for this is a vital lead to following the Lord more nearly.

Our Father, we acknowledge that we are part of your great family of nations and, as such, we must give thought to and, wherever possible, care for those within your family who suffer at the hands of others who do not follow you at all.

As we remember the atrocities that are carried out by some people, we pray with all our hearts that those evils may vanish and that your kingdom may indeed come and your will be done throughout the world. We know what a big prayer this is, Lord, but we know, too, that if peace is to come, then we must let it begin in our own lives.

We pray that everywhere your name may become honoured, and as we do so, we pray for those who leave their own country to go into dangerous areas to take the good news of Jesus to people who do not know him.

Living in a land of relative plenty, we pray, our Father, that you will show us how we can help to alleviate the hunger and thirst of those who suffer starvation and neglect. Show us how we can work alongside them that they may learn better ways of making provision for their families.

Forgive us, Lord, our sins of apathy about the world's needs, and our self-centredness that leads to neglect. If we remember harm done during wartime, or in travels, help us to rid ourselves of bitterness and, in some small way, show the kind of love we expect you to show to us.

Looking at these windows dedicated to the prisoners of conscience, we pray for those who have been brought to such severe testing. Give them strength, Lord, that their endurance may be a Christian witness to those who torment them.

What we have prayed for the family of nations, we pray too for our own relationships. Make us always aware of the needs of loved ones, help us to keep in peace with them, and may your name be honoured in our homes. Let us be willing to show hospitality, make us quick to forgive. Let our homes be filled with love, peace and joy.

We acknowledge your might, your power, your glory and pray that we may send the message around the world that you are almighty God, to be followed and obeyed more nearly day by day.

We say 'Amen', Lord God, knowing you are faithful to hear and answer our prayers according to your perfect will.

We leave the cathedral by the north porch and walk across the green to see a bronze statue called the Walking Madonna. This is an unusual portrayal of Mary and very arresting, for she is seen striding along as a determined young woman, perhaps on her way to visit her relative Elizabeth, as told in the Gospel story. At the time of her astonishment at what she had been told about giving birth to Jesus, she turned to a member of her family to share her news.

The idea of the family began with a man and a woman, and their children. It was intended that the family should be united, and that sense of unity has been with us in this cathedral as we have joined in prayer.

19

GUILDFORD

Let the young come

Guildford Cathedral is young by any standard. It is the only new Anglican cathedral to have been built in the southern province of the Church of England during the twentieth century, and one of only two on a new site in England since the Middle Ages. It was consecrated in 1961. For all that, though, it cannot be said to be entirely modern in style. The seven pointed arches reflect a Gothic style, and prove that a traditional type of building is acceptable in the twentieth century. The piers of the arches are light, the windows are mostly plain and what stained glass there is comes mainly in the form of small commemorative panels set in clear glass.

Standing at the west end of this magnificent and bright building, we can look right through to the high altar and the impressive round window with its symbol of the Holy Spirit, to whom the cathedral is dedicated, with no interruption of choir screen or organ. All this gives a sense of newness, of young life vibrating throughout. This feeling remains with us during our visit.

An appreciation of youth is found in the north ambulatory where a large framed diocesan map hangs. All the churches of the diocese are shown on the map and in their correct positions, painted in watercolours. This is the work of a schoolboy, just 17 years old at the time, who took a couple of years to finish it, working on it during his spare time. The people who serve in this cathedral consider this to be one of their most treasured possessions. It speaks to us of hope that one of the youngest Anglican cathedrals in England should attract the work of youth.

Passing from the north to the south, we look briefly into the lady chapel, which was one of the last parts of the cathedral to be built. The dark wooden statue of Madonna and child over the altar is exquisite, carved from lignum vitae, a name which means 'wood of life'.

From the chapel we move on to pause in front of the bust of the architect, Sir Edward Maufe. This is set back in a niche, but is so positioned that he appears to be looking down the length of the cathedral along the line of those soaring arches. Does he feel satisfaction as he views the building he so skilfully designed, we wonder? He should. At the far end, near the entrance, he would see the baptistry and font. Looking to the future, would his prayer be that the children baptized there would indeed become the church of the future? Sadly some will not live for the fulfilment of that vision, as we shall see.

Before moving down the south aisle, we find a small room to one side called St Ursula's Porch. This saint, who lived 1,500 years ago, is the patron saint of teachers and schoolgirls, and it is understood she had a love for children. Her statue suggests as much, for she is seen here with children gathered around her.

The place of children within the life of churches and cathedrals has changed somewhat in recent years, so the purpose of the Children's Chapel in this south aisle now has a different emphasis. Originally this small area was specifically for children's services, but now, because children and young people are included and involved in the life and worship of the cathedral, it is not considered appropriate to make separate arrangements for them.

So, this tiny chapel is being put to a very lovely use. It has been set aside specifically as a place for quietness and private prayer for bereaved parents, their relatives and friends – particularly those who have given birth to a stillborn baby or who have lost a child soon after birth, as well as those whose loss has been through miscarriage. There is a book of remembrance here, the pages of which are turned daily. Today we see the name of a little one who was just two years old when he died.

The fact that names are entered in this book is important, even though the child may never have known life after birth. The realization in recent years that this is important has been a source of comfort to parents who have suffered this kind of tragedy, for they can feel that oneness with their child that they had dreamed of having. They had borne a real person and that person had a name. Any parents wishing to record a name can ask to do so by speaking to someone on duty in the cathedral. The idea for this book of remembrance was developed by a committee in Guildford of SANDS (Stillbirth and Neonatal Death Society), and the loss of any child up to university age can be recorded. Indeed, the sorrow and grief experienced by parents and relatives has its own poignancy, aspects of it relating to the age their children were when they died.

There is a circle of chairs in the chapel and a simple altar with a cross and candlesticks. Visitors have left a variety of cards in memory of their young ones. They stand along the window ledge and in conversation with a lady worker we learn that there are always cards as well as flowers left here. The chapel is well used – a good thought but also a sad one that it is so necessary.

From our reading of the Gospels we know that Jesus loved children.

- He took a child in his arms and told his disciples that whoever welcomed one such child in his name would be welcoming him, which would also mean welcoming God, the heavenly Father.
- He called a little child to stand among the disciples and told them that they must become like that child if they were to enter the kingdom of heaven. And that whoever humbled himself like that child would be the greatest in the kingdom.
- He had harsh words to say about anyone who caused one child who believed in him to sin, saying it would be better to have a large millstone hung around their neck and be drowned.

109

- The importance Jesus placed on children comes through as we hear his words, 'See that you do not look down on one of these little ones. For I tell you that their angels in heaven always see the face of my Father in heaven.'[1]
- Children loved Jesus in return. In the story of the triumphal entry into Jerusalem on that first Palm Sunday, the children joined in with the adults, shouting, 'Hosanna to the Son of David',[2] and they would not be quietened even though the Jewish leaders tried to stop them.
- Jesus knew, too, that children were not always sweet and good. He spoke at one time of children sitting in the marketplace and grumbling because their friends would not join in their games.
- Jesus always showed special concern for children who were unwell. He went to the home of Jairus where his 12-year-old daughter was dying; he healed the epileptic son of a despairing father; he gave a healing word to an official whose son was sick.

Knowing all this, we feel a deep compassion for parents who would sit in this chapel and ask, 'Why?' Why should the baby they longed for miscarry? Why should their little one be born with no life? Why should their child die at a young age? Why should their teenagers die before they had a chance to prove their worth in society?

Outside the chapel we pass an exhibition of children's drawings. Because it is coming up to Easter, they are mostly of the cross, and there are many of them. Obviously there are many children associated with the cathedral.

Then, at the far end of this exhibition area, we come to what must surely be the most precious spot here. This is known as the Children's Window and shows Jesus with a child on his knee and others beside him, while an angel waits with another child ready to go to him. This is not the traditional picture of Jesus blessing the children of his time. Instead, the little ones in this picture are modern children, dressed in twentieth-century clothes and holding the kinds of toys children today have, such as a teddy bear. Included in the window are the well-known words of Jesus: 'Suffer little children to come unto me and forbid them not; for of such is the kingdom of heaven.'[3]

What makes this small window so special is that we do not only see it here. As we turn towards the glass doors we find it is clearly reflected with the brightness of all the colours, through them on to the stone pillars beyond. One guidebook calls it a magic window, but surely it is something more than that. Even as this picture of him with the children is transferred, by reflection, to another place, so the children lost to us in this life are transferred to his glorious presence in heaven.

Perhaps here, in this remembrance of resurrection, those who sorrow can find comfort. Through prayer, he will touch them, assuring them that his love for children did not cease when he left earth. As the picture in this beautiful little stained glass window shows, he still loves the children, he still welcomes them into his arms. More than that, we remember how, along with the children he welcomed so long ago, he also welcomed the mothers.

Looking up at the glass panel above the door here we see engraved on it an angel playing a musical instrument. There are several such engravings in the cathedral. Are they also comforting to parents, and others, who have been bereaved?

We feel a quietness as we walk down the south aisle towards the font, entering the space through wrought iron gates with the symbols of fire worked into them, reminding us that the cathedral is dedicated to the Holy Spirit. There is another reminder of this in the carvings above the travertine stone font, where three flights of seven golden-coloured doves are shown descending – another symbol of the Holy Spirit.

For some, this will be a sad place, either because their baby did not live long enough to be brought here for christening or because they lived for only a short while afterwards.

Loving Father, when we receive the gift of children, we know you give them to us to love, so it is all the more devastating when they

111

are taken from us, either before they know life on earth or at a young age. It is with difficulty that we say 'thank you' for even the brief time we have had with them.

Lord Jesus, we remember how you came to earth as a baby, born of your mother as we all are, living as a child and growing up to manhood. We thank you for this and, because of it, know you understand children.

We pray that the children we do have may come to know you and commit their lives to you while they are still young, so that they may follow you as they grow older, serving your church but above all serving you. May your Holy Spirit fill them from an early age and so help us, too, for we read in the Scriptures that a little child can lead us to you.

Lord, these days we hear much about the abuse of children, both in our own country and in countries where there is such dire poverty that they are forced into different kinds of slave labour, just to earn a meagre living. May those who grow rich out of their hard work be challenged. May those who exploit them sexually be shamed.

Forgive us, Lord, when we ignore what is happening to our children, turning blind eyes and deaf ears to their cries for help. Challenge us to follow you more nearly in our care for youngsters. Strengthen those who work in organizations that seek to give them the childhood they have so far been denied.

Lord, may all those who are growing up in an atmosphere of violence and unrest, who are refugees, who are hungry, who know no love, learn of you and your love and be blessed.

Heavenly Father, may your comfort be with all who mourn the loss of their young ones, whatever the reason – sickness, road accidents, drugs, family quarrels or violence. Bless the memories they have, and for those whose babies died before there could be any memories and whose dreams were lost, grant them your special blessing.

Amen

As we stand here looking at the symbols of the Holy Spirit, we see a somewhat deeper meaning, for this is the place of entry into the Christian Church. The Holy Spirit descending on a person indicates a receiving of that spirit which brings new birth.

Jesus told one of the Jewish leaders who was sympathetic to him that he could only see or enter the kingdom of God if he was born again. Being a 'born again Christian' is a phrase frequently used nowadays to indicate that a person has, in effect, experienced a spiritual resurrection, has become united with Jesus Christ and is trying to follow him more nearly day by day. Christ has become our Lord and Saviour, and the evidence of our rebirth is seen in the lives we lead.

20

SOUTHWARK

Never alone

Stepping into Southwark Cathedral is not like stepping into the past, for it is, and always has been, a place for today's people, a place aware of their interests, serving their daily needs. Situated as it is in the midst of London's hubbub of traffic, roadworks, warehouses, shops, offices, cafés and markets, it is somewhere for stressed city workers to pause during their lunchtime to be still, to participate in daily services or concerts of various kinds, or else to come to after work to join in Evensong. This cathedral has become part of everyday living.

This we realize as soon as we enter. Looking for the font, which is usually near a cathedral's entrance, we find that it has been moved to a more central position and in its place has been set, in the floor, a large black circular commemorative plaque to the 51 victims of the 1989 *Marchioness* disaster, the pleasure boat that sank in the nearby River Thames. Beyond, on the floor, is a square plaque listing the names of those who died. We notice that the ages, also, are given and that most were relatively young – in their twenties, and only one was over 50 years old.

As we walk along the north aisle, we pause to look at an artist's impression of a map of the diocese on the wall, a diocese where two and a half million people live. This map is dated 1987, and the general impression it gives is, again, that we are in a cathedral where today's situation is foremost in the minds of those who serve here.

Another twentieth-century tragedy has a focus in the retro-choir. Here there are four beautiful chapels, but it is the one dedicated to St Andrew that draws our attention. This thirteenth-century chapel has had a chequered history, but it can have been used for no better purpose than it is now. At an ecumenical service on World AIDS day in 1991, it was designated as a place of prayer for all those affected by HIV and AIDS. Healing services and memorial services or prayers are now held here when requested, and flowers left in memory of those who have died from an AIDS-related illness. Every Saturday the Eucharist is celebrated in this chapel.

It is quiet here, and we stand looking into the chapel towards the perpetual light burning over a memorial book. Family and friends of loved ones (of any faith or none) who have died from HIV or AIDS-related illnesses can arrange to have their names written in the book by a sister of an enclosed religious community. The light above the book not only speaks of remembrance but is also a sign of hope. And as we look at that book and the light, we cannot feel in the least judgemental about these modern sufferers, but have only a deep compassion for them. We know that our Lord would look at them and touch them with a depth of compassion we humans can never feel.

To this chapel may come those who know their lives will, tragically, be cut short by their illness, and they will feel accepted for their courage. Here may come, too, those who care for them and whose own lives will be so affected when those who suffer are gone. Those who work with the sick may come here, as can those who have been bereaved because of such illnesses. Here can be found comfort for the sufferers and challenge for those who seek to rid the world of this scourge.

There are two plaques on the wall beside the chapel that are very meaningful. They show well-known words from the Bible, but they have been so interestingly engraved that the style holds a message in itself. Behind the words 'Underneath are the' on one plaque is the rest of that text, 'everlasting arms'.[1] The other plaque comprises three texts – the words 'is love', 'is light' and 'with us' are superimposed on three repetitions of the word 'God'.

As we read the words quietly – 'God is love', 'God is light',

'God with us' – a like text comes to mind, which is equally applicable: 'God is our refuge and strength, an ever present help in trouble.'[2] It is that word 'present' that is so appropriate in this situation or, indeed, in any situation in which we humans find ourselves. The God we worship and serve is not some distant deity who has to be looked for when we meet problems. He is there already, present with us – a living God. The psalmist's words speak so clearly, even for today's world.

- Though the earth give way, God is there.
- Though mountains quake, he is there.
- Though the waters roar, he is there.
- Though illness comes – either as a result of our own folly or through no fault of our own – he is there.
- Though muggings, terrorism and vandalism continue, he is there.
- When our hearts are broken when we lose a loved one, he is there.
- When a partner proves to be unfaithful, when a child causes distress, he is there.
- When all we have worked for, all we have planned, our dearest hopes are dashed to the ground, he is there.
- When people treat us unkindly, when friends let us down, when colleagues deceive us, he is there.
- Most meaningful of all, when we are overwhelmed by sin, he is there, for he died on the cross so we might know this.
- When the time comes for us to leave this world, he is there, taking us into his presence.

Always we can know God is there – an ever present help in trouble. Once we grasp this wonderful truth, we can go on to say with confidence, as the psalmist does, 'Therefore we will not fear.'

The name given to Jesus when he came to earth comes to mind, Emmanuel, with its straightforward meaning, as portrayed on one of the plaques on the wall here: 'God with us'. Many people seem to look for God in different places and say they cannot find him. Perhaps they look too far. As the poet has said: 'Closer is He than breathing, and nearer than hands and feet.'[3] We need never be alone, whatever our situation.

Jesus himself endorsed this when he told his disciples after his resurrection, 'Surely I will be with you always, to the very end of the age.'[4] The small, delicately coloured window between the two plaques here shows Christ crowned in glory. At the bottom is the text, 'We have an advocate with the Father'.[5] How comforting it is to know that even as Jesus is always with us, he is also speaking to the Father God on our behalf.

We now move away from this poignant area and walk down the south aisle, pausing beside a memorial that, again, proves how much a part of everyday life this house of God has always been. Here is the Shakespeare Window, dedicated to our greatest English playwright, for Southwark was his parish church when he was living, writing and acting at the nearby Globe Theatre. Beneath the window lies a sculpture of the recumbent figure of Shakespeare. One panel of the window shows characters from his comedies; the other shows the tragic figures. In the central panel of the window is Prospero, the forgiving hero of *The Tempest*. Some of the words from his farewell speech are appropriate to quote here: 'And my ending is despair, unless I be reliev'd by prayer.'

People suffering from HIV and AIDS-related illnesses may well feel their ending is despair. The challenge that we must set ourselves is 'to relieve them', and all who are in distress of any kind, by means of prayer, so they may know that the God who is Love, the God who is Light, whose everlasting arms are holding them up, is the God who stays with them, right through their illness and beyond.

> *Praise to you, God, that you are Emmanuel – God with us, whether life is good or whether we are in despair.*
> *Praise to you, God, for coming to earth in the person of your son, Jesus Christ, and for his dying for all mankind on the cross, to carry our sorrows and take up our illnesses.*

Praise to you, God, for the knowledge that, whoever accepts this can know full forgiveness for all wrongs, comfort for all sorrows and assurance of life after death.

Praise to you, God, for your Holy Spirit, giving us strength to cope with whatever life flings at us, and the ability not only to cope, but to triumph over disaster and tragedy.

God, may all who suffer know you are an ever present help in their trouble, who will not only be with them to the end, but beyond this life, if they put their trust in you.

Give that faith to all who need it, and we all do.

As you are with people in their distress, show us how we may follow you by being there with them, too.

Amen

It is lunchtime as we leave the cathedral and outside the seats are full of workers sitting in the sunshine enjoying their packed lunches, feeding the birds and generally relaxing. We join them on a seat near a modern sculpture of the Holy Family – Mary, Joseph and the infant Jesus.

This cathedral is indeed a haven for tired workers, both inside and out, within the shadow of its ancient walls. Whatever their situation, he calls them to follow him more nearly, day by day.

21

EXETER

All part of the body

There is a busyness about Exeter Cathedral that is almost over-powering. We see this as soon as we approach the west front, with its numerous stone sculptures of famous kings, bishops, saints and angels gleaming in the sunshine. Watching over all from the topmost pinnacle is the stone figure of St Peter, to whom this cathedral is dedicated. The whole facade seems to be a telling of history in stone. We are, however, to find that history told in quite a different way inside.

We are greeted there by a volunteer guide who suggests that we begin our visit by just sitting and taking in the atmosphere of the cathedral. We realize later how right it is to do this because in so doing we are following the example of a lady whose work has recently become so meaningful to this place. Marjorie Dyer spent hours sitting here, living with the feel of the place, sensing its vast history and atmosphere. She did so in order to adequately design what have become known as the Exeter Rondels. These are embroidered cushions that have been added to the plinths each side of the nave. During the Middle Ages, people had to stand up during services, there being no pews or seats in the nave for the congregation. There were, however, stone benches at seat-level round the walls for elderly or ill people to sit on, which are the plinths that we see today. During the 1980s, the people of Exeter decided to add more comfortable seating to these plinths and so the cathedral authorities commissioned Marjorie Dyer to design them.

The result was the Exeter Rondels, called 'rondels' because the design consists of round shapes, the idea being that these

119

echo some of the stone carvings in the cathedral. In these round shapes have been embroidered pictures depicting scenes from Exeter's long history, starting from Roman times (about AD 300) and continuing until the present day, the last section referring to the visit of Queen Elizabeth II when she presented the Royal Maundy money.

Having sat and gazed at the vastness of the cathedral, we now walk across to the north side of the nave to begin looking at the Rondels. The skill and craftsmanship of these is so captivating that we linger beside them, almost forgetting the enormous structure we are visiting. Indeed, our eyes seem permanently lowered as we examine the tapestry-style work. There are 720 Rondels altogether in 31 sections of cushioning, carefully fitted to the plinths. The total length is about 236 feet (72 metres), and we are told that 14 million individual stitches were sewn during their making.

Not only is the history of cathedral, city, country and the world included, but interspersed is lettering featuring such scriptural passages as the opening of St John's Gospel and the Lord's Prayer. Running throughout are the words of the *Te Deum*, and the Apostles' Creed is also included. In addition, there is a thin white line in shinier thread that runs from the beginning right through to the end of the cushioning, denoting the working of the Holy Spirit through the years. The overall design is modern but simple enough that its meaning is reasonably easy to understand.

We enquire further about this magnificent piece of work and discover that it was undertaken by more than 50 members of the Exeter Cathedral Company of Tapisers over a period of five years. They worked on large embroidery frames, made by the cathedral's carpenter, and another worker had the task of coordinating all the work. Special Persian wool in 73 colours was obtained from Yorkshire, but this wool had to be reduced from three to two strands, so there had to be two wool organizers responsible for doing this. The process of research, design, construction, checking and rechecking for size, content and effect went on for months. Eventually, when the embroidery was finished, upholsterers took over to make the cushions, and they were eventually put in place in June 1989.

Although as part of our visit to this cathedral we expect to marvel at the work put into it by craftsmen over the centuries, this latest addition is what really inspires us here. Modern-day workers have given their skills to make something beautiful for this house of God, something that not only tells the history of this part of our country, but also outlines the basics of the Christian faith within that history. It is a beautiful and different kind of witness to the way in which God has been present in the lives of people of this Devon city.

More tapestry work is seen in the kneelers, set in place before each seat. These are in two series, one showing the flora of Devon, and the other musical instruments and quotes from hymns.

Music is vital to the life of this cathedral and we are particularly impressed with the minstrels' gallery, midway down the nave. Built in the fourteenth century, it is still used on special occasions. What is so attractive about it is the set of 14 carved angels, each playing a different musical instrument. Dominating the nave is the great oak organ case above the screen.

So massive is this building, and so full of history and architectural detail that it is easy to feel somewhat overwhelmed. The thought persists: how many hundreds of people have contributed to creating its beauty over the centuries, each doing his or her different part. The message of the work on the Rondels is an epitome of this idea. Designer, checkers, embroiderers, coordinator, carpenter, wool organizers, upholsterers were all needed, and they were needed for their own special talents, but worked together to produce this great work of art.

The obvious thought that comes from Scripture is the analogy the apostle Paul used to describe the Church; the body being made up of many parts, each part needed and not one dispensable: 'Now you are the body of Christ, and each one of you is a part of it.'[1] In the Church, he says, God has appointed different people for different tasks. He could not have been the first to

121

put this thought into practice.

We think about the first group of those who followed Jesus, and who were called to follow him more nearly for three years before he returned to heaven, leaving them to continue the work he had begun. They did so in the strength of the Holy Spirit.

- As this cathedral is dedicated to St Peter, we think about his place in that first disciple band of twelve men. He was obviously the spokesman for them.
- With Peter, Jesus took the fishermen brothers James and John as his companions on specially private occasions. We might today call them the committee.
- Andrew and Philip seem to have done good outreach work for it was Andrew who introduced his brother, Simon Peter, to Jesus. At the same time, Philip persuaded Nathanael to 'come and see' the kind of person Jesus was. Indeed, whenever we hear about these two, they are introducing someone to Jesus: Andrew brings a boy with five loaves and two fish to Jesus, which was the prelude to the feeding of the 5,000; together they bring a group of Greeks to Jesus because they had asked to see him. We could do with more Andrews and Philips in our churches nowadays.
- Nathanael seems to have been a quiet man, one for deep thinking – when Jesus first saw him, he was meditating under a fig tree. We need the deep thinkers, as well as people of action.
- Matthew we could almost call the secretary, as, with his writing skills – which he would have needed for his work as a tax collector – we can imagine him noting down much of what Jesus said and did, keeping a diary as it were. His Gospel gives evidence of this, with its meticulous attention to detail.
- We know that Judas Iscariot was the treasurer of the group; how tragic that he so misunderstood his master that he turned traitor. It is still sad when people fail to follow Jesus closely, not trying to understand his teaching, going their

own way; sadder still when they hold office in the Church and are poor witnesses of the Christian faith.

- The other Judas was one who did not mind asking questions, as we read in the account of the Last Supper. We can see how patient and understanding Jesus was in his replies to the disciples who wanted to understand more deeply the truths he was telling.

- It is a pity we always attach the adjective 'doubting' to Thomas because he was more than that. He was loyal, encouraging the others to go with Jesus to Bethany, even though it was a dangerous area. That they all eventually forsook Jesus and ran away when he was arrested would have troubled this man to the heart. Yet, as soon as he saw for himself the risen Lord, it was he who made the great statement: 'My Lord and my God!'[2] We should not criticize a doubter but, rather, realize that they are questioning, and that is no bad thing. Better to do so than accept whatever they are told without thinking.

- We do not seem to have any words from James, son of Alphaeus, or from Simon the Zealot, but they would each have their own part to play. In our churches we need the people who make up the main congregation, and who live out their Christian faith in their everyday living, showing that they are following Jesus more nearly.

- We cannot forget the women who, we are told, helped to support this group of early disciples and Jesus 'out of their own means'.[3] We remember, too, that it was the women who stood near the cross as Jesus died, and who were the first at the tomb on Easter morning.

Jesus had chosen these people and had a task for every one of those first disciples. They each brought their own characteristics and experiences to the work. In our Christian fellowships, we must be careful not to overlook the gifts people have that can be used in the service of the Church. Some are very noticeable, but others are not and are no less valuable for that.

It has been the designer of the Exeter Rondels whose name

123

has gone on record, yet without the embroiderers and the others who worked on her designs, we would not be seeing the result of what she felt as she sat for hours in the cathedral, absorbing its atmosphere.

One of the needlewomen has sewn her own thoughts into her work, and her words are seen in the penultimate cushion, on the south side of the nave: 'The cathedral puts into you something that you are thankful to receive, and it pulls out of you more than you thought that you possessed. G. C. C.'

As we come to worship our Lord, we are grateful for what we receive from him, but we are also challenged when he points out to us what we possess in the way of talents that can be used in his service.

Having been absorbed in examining closely the full length of the Rondels, both on the north and the south sides of the nave, we listen as a guide tells us many tales that amuse, interest and challenge. Some sadden, too, such as the way in which this great building was bombed during World War II. The tragedy struck on 4 May 1942, and the cathedral suffered a direct hit, resulting in 2,000 tons of masonry being thrown down. Fortunately, the structure itself was not affected and the repair of the damage began soon afterwards. Now it is impossible to see where that damage was, although one of the windows in the south nave aisle depicts the raid. Another states quite simply, 'This window replaces the former window destroyed by Enemy Action in May 1942.' In it we see figures of four of the saints of the early Church. Above them is the ascended and risen Christ, and below is shown a scene of the Lord with St Peter, who is kneeling at his feet. The words that are inscribed are those of Jesus, as Matthew records: 'Lo, I am with you alway'.[4]

The message of the cathedral is one of service. We have been told there are over a hundred volunteers on regular duty, acting as guides, seated at the information desk, working in the adjoining shop and refectory, as well as volunteer choristers joining the regular choir boys and organists, and the clergy who are available to speak with anyone needing help with spiritual problems.

Yet none of those workers does so in his or her own strength alone; always, Jesus himself is with them, as he is with us in our particular sphere of service. And he is always there, listening as we pray, which we do now standing before this window.

Lord, as we consider the particular role you have called us to fulfil in our Christian service, we thank you that you are always with us, giving us the strength and confidence we need for that work.

Whether we are up front, preaching or teaching, leading study groups, taking a prominent part in worship or seated in the congregation, joining wholeheartedly in that worship, giving our attention to what is being said, we pray we may do what you have apportioned to us to the best of our ability.

We humbly thank you for the privilege of serving you in whatever way you have decreed, and ask that we may be a help to both leaders and fellow Christians as we work together harmoniously.

We pray we may always remember that, as we seek to follow you more nearly day by day, you look for us to be on the alert for the ways of service you have for us to do.

Above all, may we remember why we serve you. It is as a glad response to the way in which you served us when you died on the cross to take our sins away, bringing us forgiveness and reconciliation with God, our heavenly Father.

Amen

We turn from the window, a comforting thought within us as we sense that abiding presence. Then, we glance up at one of the corbels at the top of a pillar. The colourful carving shows the figure of a man doing a handstand, watched by an angel. One of the guides tells us the story of how this man was an acrobat who joined a monastery, but as he could not sing, write books or do any of the things the other monks did, he worshipped by 'tumbling'. He found that his tricks were the best things he could do, so he offered them as his worship.

We may smile at the story, yet it has such a truth in it. When we offer to the Lord the best that we can do, he will use it. The busyness of the appearance of this cathedral shows that, over the centuries, people have done that. When we really try to discover how we are to serve the Lord, we are, in fact, relieved of the busyness because, as we dedicate our best to him and cease to strive to take on those things other people are particularly gifted to do, we can concentrate on using our own talents to the glory of our master, whom we seek to follow more nearly.

22

CANTERBURY
The welcoming Christ

If we are not too careful as we enter Canterbury Cathedral we are likely to miss something very meaningful. Stepping from the brightness outside to the more shadowy interior, looking down as we negotiate the few steps into the nave, then raising our eyes to admire the lofty grandeur of the building, and with thoughts of Thomas Becket on our minds, we may fail to see Jesus.

Just inside the south door, in the south-west porch, stands an impressive figure of Christ, carved from afrormosia wood. There is a glow behind his head and his arms are spread in welcome. It is those outstretched, welcoming arms that convey a very significant message.

This 'Mother Church of the Anglican Communion', as it is known, is so full of memorials to people from the past, so full of history, so throbbing with the story of the martyrdom of Thomas Becket and such a focal point for pilgrimage since that event that these things tend to dominate. And the saints of old would surely not have wished that, for they acknowledged and served the Lord of all, Jesus Christ, who had called them into his service.

As we stand here before this welcoming figure, so lifelike and beautiful, we think of the way in which Jesus welcomed those who came to him during his earthly ministry.

- He welcomed ordinary working men to assist him in his ministry, men like the fishermen Simon Peter and Andrew, James and John, and a tax collector called Matthew.
- He welcomed people who came to him for healing or who were brought to him to receive his healing touch.

- He welcomed even those considered untouchable, such as leprosy sufferers.
- He welcomed mothers who wanted him to give a blessing to their children and, in doing so, welcomed the children themselves – indeed, he delighted in them.
- He welcomed women who wanted to talk with him, something Jewish men did not do in those days.
- He welcomed those who were mourning the loss of loved ones or who were anxious about the health of loved ones.
- He welcomed people who were mentally ill.
- He welcomed rich people, poor people, those who were hungry, thirsty, troubled and questioning.
- He welcomed those who were despised by others.
- Above all, he welcomed those who were sinners and who knew they were.
- He even welcomed scribes and Pharisees, who considered themselves so much better than anyone else, but, unlike most others, they turned their backs on that welcome and instead arranged to have him condemned and killed.

And those welcoming arms of Jesus are still held out to all people, whatever their condition, if they will only give him their attention and not become so preoccupied with other things that they ignore him or pass him by.

We turn from the figure of Christ to make our way down into the nave, and as we get near to the beautifully carved and painted pulpit we notice a member of the clergy walking up into it. It is mid afternoon, the time for prayer, and he calls us to pause and be still. Before saying the prayers, however, he gives a sincere welcome to all visitors. We feel he has caught the spirit of that welcoming figure at the entrance.

Prayers said, we begin to move again, eager to see the place now known simply as The Martyrdom, where Thomas Becket was so savagely and wrongfully assassinated just after Christmas in 1170 by four knights serving Henry II. As we stand here before the Altar of Sword's Point, so called because over it hangs a cross made from the points of swords, we reflect that if ever there were men who were not welcomed here it would have been those four. Even Jesus did not welcome criminals if they were unrepentant. We remember, however, how he welcomed one of the thieves crucified with him, because that man acknowledged his crimes and expressed remorse for them. Surely he would have welcomed King Henry himself, too, forgiving his impetuous outburst of wanting someone to rid him of Thomas because they were in such disagreement, for he was filled with remorse that his words had been taken so literally.

Within a short time of the murder of Thomas Becket, Canterbury welcomed pilgrims from near and far who came to see this place and remember Thomas. It has welcomed them ever since. It has welcomed, too, Pope John Paul II and the then Archbishop of Canterbury, Robert Runcie, who met and prayed together at this spot in May 1982.

We go down more steps into the ancient crypt where we find peace and stillness away from the crowds in one of several chapels. The Jesus Chapel is set back a little from the massive columns that dominate this crypt and is simple and plain by comparison with some of the elaborate decorations we have seen so far. Here, thoughts of the welcome Jesus always gave are still in our minds as we recall that, after his resurrection, women, particularly Mary Magdalene, found that welcoming spirit still there. More wonderfully Peter, who had so painfully denied his Lord, experienced that welcome after a fruitless night of fishing when Jesus, in his risen form, stood on the shores of Galilee with breakfast prepared.

We leave the crypt and make our way back upstairs, then on into St Anselm's Chapel, considered by some to be the most holy place in the entire building. We understand why as we enter for, by comparison with other parts, it is, again, simple and quiet. There is just one remaining medieval painting in one corner above the altar, its strong colours showing a clear picture of the story of St Paul on the Island of Malta, and a colourful modern window dedicated to St Anselm.

This eleventh-century Archbishop of Canterbury is described

in our guidebook as 'wise and saintly, a scholar of international repute, and an undeniably cosmopolitan spirit'. From his writings, *Proslogion*, some of his words are most appropriate to remember here: 'Yield room for some little time to God; and rest for a little time in him. Enter the inner chamber of your mind; shut out all thoughts except that of God, and such as can help you in seeking him; close your door and seek him'. And in seeking we know we shall find he welcomes us.

Here is a perfect place in which to sit and pray, for this chapel is tranquil and secluded.

Lord Jesus, the welcome we have found in this great cathedral has been a comfort, but we admit it is also a challenge.

Forgive us when we do not always remember to welcome visitors into the church where we habitually worship. We realize that they may just have 'popped in' out of curiosity, because of a subconscious need, or may be lonely, newcomers to the area. Significantly, they may be seeking you. Perhaps they are a little different from ourselves, maybe they have moved here from overseas. They may not be familiar with what goes on in our church, or how they should act during worship. If they have not come to church for many years, we know you welcome them back, so help us to do so, too. Help us to see, Lord, that some of the busyness with which we surround ourselves as we come to worship is not important when set against the need to offer a simple, but not overwhelming, welcome to visitors and newcomers.

Remembering how you welcomed people in your earthly life, may we realize that in welcoming people now, we are following you more nearly.

We recognize, too, that a welcome is two-sided: a welcome extended has to be a welcome accepted for it to be complete. When we visit a church, help us to allow ourselves to be made welcome, to accept an offer of friendship and respond in like manner. Help us to overcome shyness or reserve, knowing that you, Lord, are always happy to see us in your place of worship.

We thank you, Lord Jesus, that in your human form you welcomed all who truly sought you, whatever their situation or

condition. May that memory encourage us to seek the company of
other Christian people when we move to another district or visit
another place.
Amen

Eventually we leave the main part of the cathedral, passing
between the Christ Church Gate, and look up at another figure
of the welcoming Christ. This one, a modern statue, replaces the
original that was pulled down by the Puritans. Did they not
want people to feel welcome at worship?

The message of the welcoming Christ here is really the message of all the cathedrals throughout the country. There may not
be a statue like this in every one, but his unseen presence is
there, for he is the living Lord, and his is always a welcoming
presence. He waits to welcome us all to the great houses built to
his glory, asking only that we pause while we are in them and
remember that he died for each one of us, and rose from death
so that we might know eternal life. His welcome includes a plea
that we accept and follow him more nearly day by day.

GLOSSARY

Cathedral The word comes from the Latin *cathedra*, meaning a seat or chair. A cathedral is the principal church in a diocese (an Anglican district) in which the bishop has his seat, more generally known now as his 'throne'. A cathedral is usually built in the shape of a cross, the stem lying east to west, the main part being the nave with an aisle on each side. The two arms are known as north and south transepts. At the east end, the head of the cross, are the choir and high altar. The main entrance to a cathedral is nearly always at the west end. Cathedrals and monastic churches were, in earlier days, built for the use of Christian communities where canons, monks or nuns lived. Later, many of the monastic churches also became cathedrals.

Aisle A word coming from Latin meaning 'wing' – a passage each side of the nave.

Altar An elevated structure, or table, from which the sacrament (bread and wine) is served at the Eucharist (Holy Communion). The high altar is the heart of the cathedral and the focal point for its worship.

Ambulatory A place for walking; a processional aisle usually around the east end behind the high altar.

Aumbry A small cupboard near the altar used for the storage of sacred vessels.

Boss An ornamental carving at the intersection of a vaulted roof, sometimes also painted.

Camber-beam A piece of timber cut like an arch.

Capital A moulded or carved block on top of a pillar, sometimes richly ornamented.

Chancel The eastern end of the cathedral where the choir and high altar are situated, often separated from the nave by a screen. The word means 'an enclosure'.

Chapel A small place, with an altar, for private prayer or worship.

Choir (or quire) The place where the singers and clergy sit, and where the daily worship is sung.

Choir aisle An aisle behind the area of the choir.

Choir screen A partition, often of carved lattice work, separating the choir from the main body of the cathedral.

Clerestory The upper part of the main wall, above the top of the aisled roof, with a row of windows.

Cloisters The word comes from Latin, meaning an enclosed space. It is a covered walkway alongside the exterior walls of some cathedrals, usually those that were originally monastic churches. Cloisters served as a connection between the chapter-house and other buildings, and provided a place where monks or nuns could work, have recreation and conversation. The

132

cloisters had either an open colonnade or traceried windows, overlooking an enclosed cloister garth (lawn).

Consistory court The place for an assembly or council; the court of a bishop for the trial of ecclesiastical causes.

Corbel A projecting block of timber, stone or iron to support a column, roof-rib or statue; often carved with grotesque figures.

Crossing The space formed at the intersection of nave and transepts.

Crypt A vaulted basement used for services; in earlier days it was used as a burial place beneath the chancel. The word means 'hidden'.

Fan-vaulting Elaborate carved work in the form of fans, on ceilings.

Font A basin to contain water for infant christening.

Galilee porch Porch or chapel, usually at the west end. The name suggests a meeting place (see Mark 16.7).

Hammerbeam A beam projecting from a wall to support a tie-beam.

Icon An image, or representation. A breaker of such images was known as an iconoclast.

Lantern A structure on top of a tower or roof to give light to the building's interior, and as a crowning to the fabric.

Lady chapel Usually built at the east end of the cathedral, behind the high altar, and dedicated to the Virgin Mary, who is sometimes called 'Our Lady'.

Lierne vault Stone vaulting where the main ribs are joined, or tied as it were, by small ribs crossing from one to another.

Lignum Vitae Hard, dark-coloured and close-grained wood, called 'wood of life' because of its durability.

Nave The main part of a cathedral. The name comes from the Latin for 'ship'; its shape is a reminder of an upside-down ship, the vault above usually being ship-shaped.

Pier A solid vertical mass of stone or brickwork for supporting an arch.

Pillar A slender upright structure, a column, usually circular, giving support to part of the building and capable of carrying a load.

Plinth The base of a column or wall. In earlier days the only place where sick or elderly worshippers could be seated.

Presbytery At the east end of the chancel, the sanctuary.

Reredos A screen or wall behind an altar.

Retrochoir The area behind the high altar, at the extreme east end.

Romanesque Architecture imitative of Roman, often called Norman, of the eleventh and twelfth centuries.

Rood The cross or crucifixion scene.

Sanctuary See Presbytery.

Screen A partition of stone, wood or metal separating parts of a cathedral; there is often a screen between the nave and choir.

Transept Transverse arms of a cathedral, running north and south. Usually referred to as 'north transept' or 'south transept'.

Triptych A set of three panels hinged side by side, and capable of being folded together; each panel is painted distinctively, as seen in an altar-piece.

Vault Arched roof.

NOTES

Chapter 1

1 Matthew 14.31.
2 John 11.
3 Matthew 26.42.

Chapter 2

1 Psalm 90.2.
2 Genesis 1.1
3 Hebrews 11.6.
4 Genesis 1.31.
5 Hebrews 13.8.
6 Psalm 90.12.

Chapter 3

1 Genesis 1.2 and 3.
2 The hymn by S. J. Stone (1839–1900).

Chapter 4

1 Jonah 2.9.
2 Genesis 28.17.
3 Psalm 119.105.

Chapter 5

1 John 10.11.
2 John 19.1.
3 Matthew 26.53.
4 John 10.10.
5 Isaiah 53.

Chapter 6

1 John 19.3.
2 John 12.13–15.
3 John 19.15
4 John 19.19.

5 Hebrews 2.9.

Chapter 7

1 Luke 23.28.
2 Luke 23.47.
3 'Olivet to Calvary' by Shapcott Wensley and J. H. Maunder.
4 Lamentations 1.12.
5 Matthew 16.24.
6 Matthew 10.38.
7 The hymn by William Bullock (1797–1874).

Chapter 8

1 Hebrews 7.25.
2 Matthew 11.28.
3 'And didst Thou love the race that loved not Thee' by Jean Ingelow (1820–97).

Chapter 9

1 John 3.14.
2 John 12.32 and 33.
3 Luke 23.34.
4 John 19.26.
5 John 19.28 AV.
6 John 19.30.
7 Matthew 27.46.
8 Luke 23.46
9 'When I survey' by Isaac Watts (1674–1748).

Chapter 10

1 Romans 3.23.
2 John 21.17.
3 John 8.11 AV.

Chapter 11

1 Matthew 18.10.
2 Luke 2.14.
3 Luke 23.46.
4 Psalm 150.
5 Luke 15.10.

Chapter 12

1 Luke 23.34.
2 Luke 22.42.

Chapter 13

1 'Once in Royal David's city' by C. F. Alexander (1818–95).

Chapter 14

1   Matthew 11.30.
2   'Lord of all being' by O. W. Holmes (1809–94).

Chapter 15

1   Matthew 21.15.
2   Matthew 21.16.
3   Psalm 33.1ff.
4   Psalm 150.4.

Chapter 16

1   Matthew 27.24.
2   Ephesians 6.16.
3   Matthew 27.42.
4   Matthew 27.46.
5   Philippians 3.10 and 11.

Chapter 17

1   2 Corinthians 3.18.
2   Galatians 5.22 and 23.

Chapter 18

1   Mark 11.17.

Chapter 19

1   Matthew 18.10.
2   Matthew 21.9.
3   Mark 10.14 AV.

Chapter 20

1   Deuteronomy 33.27.
2   Psalm 46.1.
3   'The Higher Pantheism' by Alfred, Lord Tennyson (1809–92).
4   Matthew 28.20.
5   1 John 2.1 AV.

Chapter 21

1   1 Corinthians 12.27.
2   John 20.28.
3   Luke 8.3.
4   Matthew 28.20 AV.